Get your " " bonuses (worth over $100.00) when you get this book...

When you buy "How to Be the Bad Boy Women Love" you are eligible for special extra "Hard to Get Man" bonuses, including... *How to Do Your First "Disconnect" with a Hot Woman*

This bonus "break-out session" will take you by the hand and walk you step-by-step through doing your FIRST disconnection with a woman.

This special report and 2 downloadable audios covers...

* Overcoming the myths that stop you from using disconnectors with hot women;

* Real-world examples of successful "first disconnections" with hot women;

* How to prepare yourself for doing your first disconnector with hot women;

* Handling her reaction to your disconnection;

... and more.

You'll also get access to other special info and updates!

Once you've got the book, grab yours by going to

HTTP://HOWTOSUCCEEDWITHWOMEN.COM/HTG2222840.HTML

HOW TO BE THE BAD BOY WOMEN LOVE

GETTING HOT WOMEN TO PURSUE YOU BY BEING A "HARD TO GET" MAN

RON LOUIS & DAVID COPELAND

MASTERY TECHNOLOGIES PRESS

For tons of great info on getting what you want with women, both through connecting and disconnecting, visit http://howtosucceedwithwomen.com.

Email us at info@howtosucceedwithwomen.com

DISCLAIMER:

Having said that, welcome to becoming a Hard to Get Man! Have fun!

Ron Louis & David Copeland

TABLE OF CONTENTS

CHAPTER 1

BNB

INTRODUCTION

Guys ask us all the time what are the most important skills they need to learn to succeed with women. What do we tell them, you ask? How to jerk off with your left hand? No. How to get a phone number from a supermodel while she is hailing a cab? No way. How to bust into a porn convention and get a porn star to blow you in a closet? As cool as the BJ would be, the answer is still **no**. How to get a woman to have philosophical discussions on the meaning of life? Are you nuts? No way!

The real skills you need to master for a lifetime of success with women is the ability to **connect** with women and **disconnect** with women. Just connecting will not produce sexual feelings or true attraction. If you only connect with women it will create friendship and trust, but most likely she will also shove you into the friendship zone. If you only disconnect with women you will cause some sexual tension, but not enough trust, as a result a woman will most likely feel turned off. You need both connection and disconnection to truly master the art of dating, and that's what this book is all about.

We have a confession to make. When we wrote *How to Succeed with Women* nearly ten years ago, we thought that creating deep rapport and a deep connection was the only way to get a woman into bed. And sometimes it works. We've both had our share of hot babes that we met using our methods. We later learned that we could succeed with many **more** women by mastering the art of connection and disconnection.

After working with thousands of men in person in our coaching program, we've found that they need to master both creating rapport with women and also finding ways to demonstrate how they are different from women. In fact, we've found that our most successful students are masters at both connection and disconnection. We finally decided to share with you the material we've previously only taught at our seminars and to our private coaching clients to you.

In this book we'll share with you tips on how to be a bad boy, how to be charismatic, and how to be wildly successful with women. We are going to impart to you the blueprint for mastering connection and disconnection and show you how to become a Hard to Get Man in the process.

WHAT IS A BNB?

Lets face it: most guys fail with women. And they don't just fail occasionally with women. They fail over and over again. Do you know a guy who repeatedly fails with women? Imagine him for a second there in front of you. What are some examples of the stupid shit he does over and over again?

Men who fail with women tend to share certain characteristics. These tendencies are present across the spectrum of men of all age groups, degrees of geekiness, and shapes and sizes.

You could sum up what most men do as acting like a BNB.

BNB stands for a **Boring Nervous Bonehead**, and most guys act like a BNB around women.

Most guys act boring, dress boring, use boring and predictable lines with women, talk about boring things, and as a result women are turned off.

Most guys also are nervous and fearful around women. They're scared of approaching, talking to, connecting to, and dealing with women. Scared of rejection, being laughed at, or just fearful in general.

And guess what? Women can spot a nervous guy a mile away. He telegraphs fear in everything he does, and then women are forced to reject him. The BNB talks too fast, uses nervous movements when he talks, and he looks scared shitless.

Here is what the BNB is afraid of being: raw, real, messy, passionate, opinionated, emotional, and intense.

NOT TAKING ENOUGH RISKS

Here's an example of someone who's willing to take a risk in showing who he is and how he acts. It's from the movie *Jay and Silent Bob Strike Back*:

> "I am the master of the C.L.I.T. Remember this fucking face. Whenever you see C.L.I.T., you'll see this fucking face. I make that shit work. It does whatever the fuck I tell it to. No one rules the C.L.I.T. like me."—JAY, *Jay and Silent Bob Strike Back*

Jay is not boring. He's a lot of things, but he's not boring. We offer the example of Jay to get you to wake up. Wake up and notice that the ways you've been acting around women have been boring and predictable.

The first characteristic of BNBs is that they are **boring!** They ask boring questions, they do predictable things, and they take very few actual risks with women. BNBs telegraph that they are boring by dressing boring, by acting like every other guy does being overly compliant, not getting too close to a woman when he talks to her—and by being so amazed when a woman does actually reciprocate in a conversation that he becomes a submissive puppy dog.

BNBs never have the balls to take any romantic or sexual risks when they meet women. We're not talking about going up and grabbing some random woman's tit either. We're talking about the inability to ask for a number, give a compliment, give a woman shit, bust her on her bad behavior, or share an intense emotion. Taking a risk means doing something unpredictable—even if it might risk rejection, looking stupid, making mistakes, offending a woman, or even being uncomfortable.

In this book we'll show you exactly how to take risks with women.

THE BNB WILL TAKE ANY WOMAN

Imagine if you had no standards when it came to buying a car. You might accept anything from a total piece of shit 1993 Ford Taurus Station Wagon to a 2006 Ferrari 360 Spider. Is there a difference? Both will get you where you want go, right? But they are totally different. If you are selective about the car you drive, why not apply this same selectivity to the women you date?

The BNB has no standards when it comes to dating. The problem is that he will take any woman who shows up in his life and as a result he gets **no** women. If you want to be powerful with women, you'd better have standards. You also need to devise a way to test the women you meet. If you are serious about being a Hard to Get Man, you'd better start right now having self-respect and being willing to test women to find the one you actually like and are attracted to. We'll cover this in greater depth in the next chapter.

THE SNAVE: THE SNIVELING SNOTBAG

There is even a form of the BNB far worse than just the normal boneheaded guy. This guy is the liar, the whiner, the fuckhead, the guy you do not want to become. The SNAVE is the guy who is too stuck to even try anything with women. His excuse? "Nothing will ever work." And as a result of his attitude, this guy is angry at the world and endlessly complains like a bitch. Perhaps this type of BNB has gone so long without getting laid that he has become bitter and his lack of sex has made him nuts.

TAKE THIS TEST TO FIND OUT IF YOU ARE A HARD TO GET MAN

QUESTION #1:

You meet a woman at a party and get her phone number, what do you do?

POSSIBLE ANSWERS:

a. If you call the woman back, but really don't want to, you are an Easy to Get Man. If you feel obligated to go after any woman who will have you and feel as though you have no say in the process you are definitely an Easy to Get Man.

b. If you simply do not call the woman back because you feel it's not worth it and come up with reasons why she gave you her number, but doesn't like you, you're an Impossible to Get Man.

c. If you call the woman because you genuinely want to and made an actual connection, you're a Hard to Get Man. The Hard to Get Man doesn't do things out of obligation or out of being a nice guy. He goes after what he wants and enjoys the process.

QUESTION #2:

She talks about sex, and pushes her tits and leans into you.
You really want to move in for the first kiss, what do you do?

POSSIBLE ANSWERS:

a. The Easy to Get Man acts like a BNB. In other words, he tells the woman how hot she is and how special she is. He begins supplicating her and basically begging her for sex. Or, he is so caught up in trying to be nice and act perfectly that he does nothing, but kicks himself about it later.

b. The Impossible to Get Man feels as though the woman is only teasing him, so he gives her a disgusted look and walks away. Or, he tells her that if he kisses her then she has to go home with him.

c. The Hard to Get Man loves sex and enjoys the process. He knows that sexual and sensual "play" is part of the seduction process. So he plays along and pushes things at his speed. If he gets tired of her he walks away. If he feels a connection he pushes for more: getting her phone number or scoring with her that night. The Hard to Get Man might even be totally honest with the woman and tell her that he is nervous about approaching her, confessing how attractive he finds her. He takes risks in anything he does, however. The Hard to Get Man is above all **not** needy and not desperate.

QUESTION #3:

A woman overhears you talking about sex. She makes a silly-but-judgmental comment. Do you talk to her, avoid her, or do you apologize?

POSSIBLE ANSWERS:

a. The Easy to Get Man apologizes immediately and is overly concerned with not offending the woman. He smiles nervously and then finally says, "You are really attractive, let me buy you a drink." He then proceeds to talk about safe and boring things until she gets disgusted and walks away.

b. The Impossible to Get Man, who is naturally defensive, assumes she is an angry feminist and tells her to go away. He then avoids her.

c. The Hard to Get Man sees her comments as an invitation to play. He makes a silly comment back and challenges her, in a flirty way. The Hard to Get Man asks her about her crazy sexual experiences in life and other questions he is genuinely curious about. She laughs and they talk more. He then uses Sexual Teasing with her (you will learn this in the Tools section). And then they end up making out in a corner.

QUESTION #4:

You meet a woman at a coffee shop, you ask her out and she wants you to take her to an expensive sushi place. What do you do?

POSSIBLE ANSWERS:

a. The Easy to Get Man obviously does it, because he often gives things he doesn't want to give to women and as a result is frequently taken advantage of.

b. The Impossible to Get Man tells the woman to "fuck off" and stops calling her or interacting with her.

c. The Hard to Get Man does what he wants to do. If he only wants to set up a coffee date he does that. If he feels more comfortable just going out for drinks he suggests that instead. If he thinks paying for dinner is premature, he tells her "no" and counteroffers something else instead. Above all, he does not sell himself out or placate a woman just to get her to go out with him. At the same time he isn't rude or nasty about it.

QUESTION #5:

A woman is rude to you; do you keep talking to her?

POSSIBLE ANSWERS:

a. The Easy to Get Man does keep talking to her. He is so excited that a woman shows any interest in him that he keeps right on talking.

b. The Impossible to Get Man, always up for a fight, immediately tells the woman to go away and walks away.

c. The Hard to Get Man "busts" the woman. He asks her why she is being rude. Or he asks why her parents never taught her to be polite to strangers. The Hard to Get Man does not put up with nasty behavior, but is able to be playful back, thus giving her an opportunity to redeem herself and soften. If she plays back he will enjoy talking to her further. If she continues to be mean he will either leave, or use some of the shit-giving techniques we will be teaching you in a later chapter.

QUESTION #6:

You are having a great time talking to a woman at a coffee shop. She says something you totally disagree with, and you're actually a bit offended by her comments. What do you do?

POSSIBLE ANSWERS:

a. The Easy to Get Man avoids conflict no matter what. He believes that if he is always nice and agreeable, women will eventually like him and sleep with him. He tries his best to "match and mirror" women and do everything he can to create rapport with women. As a result, in this situation, the woman has no respect for him and his chances of sex greatly decrease.

b. The Impossible to Get Man pushes the woman and tells her all the ways she is wrong. He attacks her position so intensely that she begins crying and runs out of the coffee shop.

c. The Hard to Get Man knows that having contrasting opinions is important in dealing with women. He is totally honest with the woman and tells her that what she said offended him.

After speaking his truth she apologizes and they talk about something else and later exchange numbers. The Hard to Get Man accepts that his opinions and views may be different than a woman's. He doesn't avoid conflict or disagreement. In fact, he knows that one component of being Hard to Get is expressing contrasting opinions and differences.

WHAT IS AN EASY TO GET MAN?

The Easy to Get Man will take any woman that he can. His desperation leads him to basically hook up with any chick that is breathing. The Easy to Get Man has no self-respect, nor does he have the balls to go after what he wants.

Here is what the Easy to Get Man does:

He gives things he doesn't want to give.
He does things he doesn't want to do.
He offers things he doesn't want to offer.
He agrees with things he doesn't agree with.

✳ **The Easy to Get Man often falls into the trap of thinking that he can buy himself a woman** or that paying for expensive dates, etc. will impress a woman. Instead, he is often taken advantage of and used by women.

✳ **The Easy to Get Man is afraid to say "no" to women** because he fears he'll end up alone. Instead, he just sells out and gives away his power to every woman he meets.

✳ **The Easy to Get Man placates women.** By placating, we mean he puts women on a pedestal and acts as though women are better than him. Therefore, the Easy to Get Man assigns a woman more value than he assigns himself. It conveys that he is of lower status than she is.

✳ **The Easy to Get Man falls into the category of "nice guy"** and ends up in the friend category by not being able to put out sexual or romantic vibes.

✳ **The Easy to get Man fears expressing anything romantic or sexual** to a woman because he is afraid that if a woman knows he's sexually interested she will no longer like him. The Easy to get Man will also hang out with a woman for weeks or more hoping that things will get sexual even though there is not even a slight interest on her part that things will get sexual.

✳ **The Easy to Get Man thinks that even hanging out as her therapist or "pal" is better than being alone,** but he often ends up frustrated that no woman will have a sexual relationship with him. (See our *Nice Guy Syndrome* course to find out more on how to overcome being a nice guy. http://howtosucceedwithwomen.com/shy)

✳ **The Easy to Get Man squelches his own opinions, thoughts, feelings, and ideas** around women in a disgusting attempt at being more "agreeable." He does things like avoiding disagreements or changing his opinions to match a woman, or he even lies about himself to impress a woman more. He will also give compliments on things he could care less about or goes to "chick flick" movies when he secretly hates them.

* **The Easy to Get Man thinks that if he can prove that he is exactly like any woman he meets then she will like and accept him.** Instead, the opposite happens. Women find him boring, tame, and wimpy. In short, he agrees with things he doesn't agree with and sells out around women.

* **The Easy to Get Man avoids conflict at any cost.** He will do things like put up with disrespectful behavior from a woman out of fear of losing her. The Easy to Get Man takes a lot of shit from women and tolerates it. He will screw up his schedule to do things on her time frame rather than his. Rather than breaking up with a woman, speaking up, or cutting a woman out of his life, he keeps on tolerating insults, rude behavior, and bullshit.

Ultimately this type of man ends up resenting his life and resenting women for taking advantage of him.

WHAT IS AN IMPOSSIBLE-TO-GET MAN?

* **The Impossible to Get Man does his best to push women away.** Everything to the Impossible to Get Man is either black or white—with nothing in between. So he is always judging himself and women against an impossible standard. Women, in

his experience, are either super hot or ugly bitches—nothing in between. He meets a woman and she is either amazingly cool or a total boring jerk. He either has the perfect opening line or is dumbfounded as to what to say.

✳ **To the Impossible to Get Man, a woman either shows total respect to him or he feels that she is a nasty, disrespectful bitch.** If he is out on a date with a woman and she answers her cell phone, for example, he will yell at her, "You bitch, what do you think I am, your damn doormat. Don't you ever disrespect me like that again or we're through." Or online, when a woman is hesitant to exchange phone numbers, he might write her, "Look you hole, I'm not some puppy dog you can push around. You either give me your number or never write me again."

✳ **The Impossible to Get Man has a version of the Napoleon Complex**—a sort of inferiority complex whereby someone compensates for feeling inferior to others by trying to act ultra tough, mean, and intimidating. The Impossible to Get Man tries to act "cocky and funny," even though on the inside he feels weak, small, uninteresting, and awkward.

So, do you think this guy meets a lot of women? Do women or men even enjoy being around a man like this? When you have acted like this, how did it feel?

✳ **The Impossible to Get Man is so caught up in protecting himself that he takes no risks with women.** Risking with women would ultimately mean letting go of the "tough guy" act and exposing his vulnerability. Instead, The Impossible to Get Man complains like a bitch and acts angry to everyone around him. He also has the "victim" mentality, which makes him look like a whiney little girl. We've all met guys like this and they are exhausting to be around.

Our experience in coaching guys like this is that they are a miserable bunch. Nothing ever works out for them and they come across as angry, bitter, and nasty. Trust us, we've seen **a lot** of these guys pass through our seminars during the past ten years, and luckily we're among the few people out there who know how to work with men like this.

WHAT IS A HARD TO GET MAN?

You now know about the Easy to Get Man and the Impossible to Get Man. So, what is the Hard to Get Man like? We will cover that right now. You already have some idea of the Hard to Get way through our test analysis, but now we will teach you the specific characteristics of a Hard to Get man.

The Hard to Get Man Follows
the Charismatic Model

The Charismatic Model combines four essential qualities. The Hard to Get Man knows how to express all of these qualities with women.

One part of the Charismatic Model is the ability to be kind, warm, and caring about people and the world.

A second part of the model is the ability to be sensual and romantic. This part involves talking about romantic things, seeing romantic details, and relating on a sensual and sexual level with women.

The third part of the Charismatic Model is the ability to be playful, silly, and fun.

The fourth component is the ability to walk away from women, to be tough, to not take any shit, and to be courageous.

As you can see, if you only have one of these qualities you can easily fail with women, but when all of them are operating at once you are **unstoppable**. (To learn the specifics on how to put these qualities into practice with women, see our Advanced Course.)

What the Hard to Get Man does:

✳ **The Hard to Get Man is willing to walk** away from a woman if she is rude to him. He doesn't sell out or give his balls away to women. He has high self-regard and only gives when he wants to give.

✳ **The Hard to Get Man is an excellent communicator.** He is able to tell the truth about what he thinks, feels, experiences, etc. We will cover how to communicate like a Hard to Get Man later in this book.

✳ **The Hard to Get Man is not ashamed of his sexual desires.** He is able to flirt romantically. He is able to have fun effortlessly talking to women about sexual and sensual things.

✳ **The Hard to Get Man does not placate women.** He has high self-respect and doesn't do things he doesn't want to do. He doesn't sell out around women or feel as though he has to lie to or manipulate women.

Being a Hard to Get Man is about enjoying life on your own terms. It's about being a good guy, yet not being a wimpy guy who feels as if he has to take shit from women. It's a balance. It's about enjoying women, and not feeling compelled to impress them or to be overly aggressive.

Being Hard to Get is about being responsible for your life, not being a whining baby.

Being Hard to Get is about being selective, having criteria, maintaining high standards, taking risks, and getting a lot of women.

✳ **A Hard to Get Man works the fundamentals of dating and seduction.** He understands that successfully seducing women is like any other long-term project. He understands that, at first, he will have to put a lot of energy into it, and settle for small results until he gets better at it. He knows that at the beginning of learning any new skill there is a lot of work, and that the returns at first are small. He understands that returns get larger only as his skill level increases, which will only happen with practice.

The Hard to Get Man understands the fundamentals of seduction, and he practices the fundamentals on a daily basis. He knows that only by mastering the fundamentals can he become a more effortless and effective seducer.

THE HARD TO GET MODEL

The Hard to Get Model is a way of life. It's a combination of behaviors, attitudes, skills, and ideas that combine to create an attractive man. When you combine these qualities with the

Charismatic Model, you have a man who lives life on his terms and is irresistible to women.

This is what the "bad boy" does that makes him so irresistable to women. And it's what you'll do, once you know how to be a Hard to Get man.

Passion and Intensity

Passion is power. The Hard to Get Man is passionate about life. He has energy and passion about things **other** than women in his life. Being passionate is demonstrated in having **energy** and showing passion in conversations.

The BNB is predictable and flat, boring, and lame. Intensity is about being focused, having strong opinions, and being unashamed of your passions. A leader. Someone who is up to stuff and you want to be up to stuff with them. Someone with their own style.

Drama

Women love drama, and in case you haven't noticed, they create drama in all aspects of their lives. Drama means having things unfold like they do in a movie—an emotional tale with dramatic ups and downs and a variety of experiences and emotions through conversations, stories, or events.

Mystery, Complexity, and Depth

Predictability is boring. Women crave men who can create interesting conversations, which make them work hard to find meaning and answers.

Women crave men who are complex and deep. They want a man who can talk about a variety of subjects in depth and demonstrate originality and uniqueness in his personality. In our live seminars, we spend days exploring ways to demonstrate an interesting personality based on the stories you tell and the things you talk about.

A mysterious person doesn't tell everything up-front, and they have more to them than meets the eye. They are not exactly secretive, but they are hard to understand, pigeonhole, or entirely figure out.

Chaotic, Unpredictable, Flexible Behavior

The Hard to Get Man is unpredictable in the things he talks about, the way he behaves, and the way he expresses himself. As a result the Hard to Get Man is flexible in his approach with women and is able to deal with the inherent chaos involved in relating to women.

You really cannot predict how a conversation with a woman will go. The BNB wants everything to be nice, orderly, safe, and predictable. The Hard to Get Man, however, knows that interacting with women is chaotic, messy, and sometimes crazy. The only thing predictable about interacting with women is that it's never the same way twice.

You might, for example, be having a great conversation with a woman about vacation spots or her favorite restaurants, and then she begins to cry thinking about a former boyfriend or a pet who recently died. The BNB freaks out and thinks her expression of strong emotions is bad and ruining his seduction. The Hard to Get Man goes with it. He pushes into the sadness, he is able to relate to strong emotions, and he shares strong emotions with the woman. In our Advanced Course we walk you through, step-by-step, how to speak emotionally and relate emotionally to women. For now, you just need to be aware of adding more unpredictability to your behavior, and doing the steps we'll outline in this book.

Again, the Hard to Get Man has trained himself to deal with chaos and to be comfortable with chaos. He acts in unpredictable ways and is comfortable with the ways women act impulsively. He is able to do unpredictable things such as jumping up in the middle of a conversation and tickling a woman, or talking about metaphysical topics in the middle of a conversation about sports.

Fun and Exciting

If you are serious about succeeding with women you better be fun to be around. Think this through rationally, bro. Do you honestly think anyone wants to be around a depressing guy who never smiles or who scowls anytime anyone tells a joke? Do you think chicks want to be around a low-energy guy who is boring, humorless, and seems angry and/or closed? No pickup lines or fancy patterns will help you if you're not fun to be around. There is no way you are going to find, meet, or keep a woman in your life if you are not fun and exciting to be around.

We're not saying you need to act like a clown or a comedian either. If you are not naturally funny, don't start now. There is nothing worse than someone telling stupid jokes, and then making it worse by fucking up the delivery. But if you are naturally funny and are just shy, stop holding back. Let it out.

Being fun means being relaxed, easy to be around, enjoying hanging out with women, appreciating humorous stories, being open about your life and your experiences.

What else does it mean to be fun? It means being playful. It means being silly. It means enjoying the time with a woman and being enjoyable to be around.

A Hard to Get Man Does Not Avoid Conflict and Has an Edge

Most guys avoid conflict with women like the plague. Anytime a conversation gets heated a BNB does everything he can to avoid a disagreement or a conflict. He will apologize, change the subject, or get incredibly scared.

The Hard to Get Man doesn't avoid conflict. He pushes women to find their "hot" buttons. He knows that conflict is seductive. Yes, read it again: conflict can be seductive to women. Conflict is bonding. Conflict presents a challenge for a woman. Conflict shows you have self-respect and do not take shit. And conflict invokes emotional passion from women, which often evolves into sexual energy. Think about how hot sex can be after a couple makes up after a fight. Later in this book we will teach you specific tools that will teach you techniques for creating conflicts with women.

By "edge," we mean that the Hard to Get Man talks about unusual topics and pushes the envelope with women. He stretches the limits in a conversation by bringing up challenging topics. By "edge," we refer to talking about things that might upset a woman or put her off.

CHAPTER 2

Why a Man Who Will Take "Any Woman" Always Goes Home Alone— And How You Can Use Testing and Disqualifying Women to Become Hard to Get

Take this pop quiz, hot shot:

Which of these businesses do you think is more successful?

Business #1: A business where the owners believe that their product is for "everyone," and who pursues all people equally, as potential customers, or

Business #2: A business where the owners focus on disqualifying most people—the "non-buyers"—as quickly and efficiently as they can, and who lavish their attention on a small, tightly targeted subsection of the marketplace that is full of potentially rabid, enthusiastic customers.

It's an old business-school question, and the answer, it turns out, is always the same:

The business that disqualifies non-buyers quickly, focusing only on connecting with those customers who bring in the most profit, will make the most money.

To most people it seems like Business #1 would be more successful: after all, if you only manage to sell your product to 1% of everyone, that's a lot of money! Surely, such businessmen think, you want to throw as wide a net as possible.

It's not true. In fact, a business that tries sell their product to everyone will be out of business in no time.

It's Business #2—the one that disqualifies the nonbuyers and focuses **only** on the customers it wants—is the one that will make significantly more money, even if it's going after fewer potentials.

So why are we telling you this?

We are telling you this because, when it comes to women, most BNBs are just like Business #1.

They think that if they go for **every** attractive woman, and never risk "closing the door" on any of them, they are more likely to succeed.

But that's as wrong in dating as it is in business.

Here's the ghastly, shocking truth:

If you are looking for "any woman," you will always go home with "no woman."

A man who knows how to be Hard to Get with women gets women. A man who will take "any attractive woman" doesn't get women. And that's the end of the story.

We can hear you saying, "But I'm Hard to Get with women already! In fact, I only want to date a supermodel, but I don't even talk to them! In fact, if a woman is at all hot, I totally avoid her! Isn't that enough to Hard to Get?"

The answer is **no.** You aren't being Hard to Get. You're just taking yourself out of the game. You are, in effect, being impossible to get. That is totally different from what we are talking about, as you will see.

And maybe you're also worrying in the following manner: "Won't disqualifying women leave me with only the fat, ugly ones to chose from?" Again, the answer is **no.** In fact, Hard to Get actions work even **better** on hot women.

Look, hot women know they are hot. They have dozens of men telling them so everyday. In fact, faced with a hot woman, 99.99% of men's testing and disqualifying circuitry goes offline immediately. They'd do anything—and we mean **anything**—to get that woman into bed. Most men have no judgment whatsoever.

That's where you can be different. By being willing to be Hard to Get with women—first by testing and disqualifying them, and then later by applying the other tools we'll teach you in this book— you'll be in that .01% of men who actually present a fascinating challenge to super-hot women. And, as you'll see, presenting such a challenge is a very good idea indeed.

WHAT BEING HARD TO GET DOES

✳ **Being Hard to Get filters out the women who are basically not seducible.** Just as a smart business filters out the potential customers who will probably never buy, the smart seducer filters out the potential women who will probably never actually put out sexually.

✳ **Being Hard to Get helps you focus on your actual prospects.** Like we said, this does **not** mean the fat and ugly ones; in fact, those women usually get disqualified first. If you can accept that focusing your attention on the women who are seducible will increase your pull rate, you'll never have to be alone again.

* **Being Hard to Get begins the seduction process.** Remember: women—like all people—want what is rare, in demand, or difficult to get. When you are Hard to Get, you show that the valuable commodity is you, not her, which immediately starts the process of the seduction.

* **Being Hard to Get gives you a lot more energy for the women who "make the cut."** Just as businesses that only focus on a tightly selected group of customers have more energy and focus to spend courting those potentials, when you quickly get rid of the women who would never put out, you are able to focus like a laser on the women who might—and that leads to a lot more success.

* **Being Hard to Get women shows that you are a man who is willing to walk from the seduction.** It "sets the stage" for the seduction to be on your terms, not hers. Being Hard to Get shows that you, and your attention, is a limited quantity that she might miss out on if she doesn't play her cards right.

* **Being Hard to Get makes you interesting to women.** As we said, every hot woman is surrounded by herds of guys who

would be willing to do anything, no matter how humiliating, to get her in bed. While you might find it hot to be desired by lots of women, so much groveling attention disgusts a woman who wants to be with a strong, masculine, interesting guy. If you are a Hard to Get Man, you become one of the few men who is actually interesting to hot women.

There is one more core skill you have to have if you are going to be Hard to Get, and you must know it before we teach you the Hard to Get moves themselves.

THE CORE SKILL YOU MUST HAVE TO BE HARD TO GET WITH WOMEN

Imagine this: There you are, sitting in a coffee shop, and a hot woman sits down at the table next to you. You really want to talk to her. What's the most important skill you **must have** to get that interaction started?

Is it knowing a bunch of really great opening lines?

No.

Is it having at your disposal a truckload of different seduction gambits, openings, NLP, tricks and ploys?

No.

Is it being a great performer? Or being really physically attractive? Or being exactly what she thinks she's looking for in a man?

No, no, and no.

Is it wearing pheromone cologne? Playing subliminal music?

No and no again.

In fact, it's none of the things that most men think it is.

Here's the one thing you must have to make that interaction work—and if you don't have it, the interaction will never work, no matter what you do have:

YOU MUST HAVE THE ABILITY TO TAKE SOME RISK

It's like we said in Chapter 1. If you can't take a risk, it doesn't matter how many seduction techniques you know. Because if you can't take a risk, you can't use any of them.

Now before you freak out about having to take risks with women, let us reassure you.

We are **not** telling you that you have to make a fool of yourself. You don't have to.

We are **not** telling you to put yourself in scary situations with women, with no idea how to handle yourself. You don't have to do that, either.

And we are **not** telling you that you have to take huge risks with hot women. In fact, we emphatically say you should **not** take huge risks.

So calm down, because this is actually good news. Once you understand how to take simple, small, appropriate risks with women, you'll be able to leave the world of the BNB and start having relationships with hot women.

IS BEING HARD TO GET WITH WOMEN RISKY?

Often men we work with will tell us that they think that being Hard to Get with women is risky.

Let's take a look at some of the common risks that men think being Hard to Get involves:

COMMONLY VOICED RISK #1: "If I am Hard to Get with women, none will be left over, and I'll never get laid!"

Men who worry about this are afraid that if they close off potential women they could have sex with (by being Hard to Get), then they will end up alone. "How do I know which women will say yes to me?" they often ask. "I'm better off keeping all my options open."

A successful seducer stays "in the game"—which most BNBs aren't able to do—and at the same time is Hard to Get with women. When you take Hard to Get actions properly, it keeps you interacting with women, while at the same time giving them a reason to pursue interacting with you.

COMMONLY VOICED RISK #2: "If I am Hard to Get with women, women might think I'm insulting them, and they may not like me, and so I'll never get laid."

It is true that you will be less likable to some women if you use our techniques. Please remember this: While a Hard to Get Man does not set out to be disliked, at the same time "being liked" is not his goal. (Being liked is the BNB's goal, and you know how badly that is working.) Being interesting, intriguing, and compelling are the Hard to Get Man's goals.

The thing is, there will be times when the hot woman you are interacting with needs to be put in her place and "brought down a notch." We'll get into the terribly, terribly wrong ways that BNBs do that, and show you how to do it properly when a woman needs it.

In those instances when you need to show a woman that you won't tolerate her bad behavior, she may not like you. She may get angry or upset. That can certainly happen.

But when you "bust" a woman according to the way we recommend, two things can happen:

First, you may find that she becomes attracted to you. You've no doubt noticed that hot women are disgusted by men who won't stand up for themselves. In fact, many hot women test men to see if they will stand up for themselves, and the men who fail to— that is, almost all of them—never get past their first sentence with her.

As we'll discuss in detail later in this book, conflict can be seductive to a woman, if done properly. So you may find, as our students often do, that a woman opens up and softens considerably after you take a testing and disqualifying action. You've become interesting and worthy of her pursuit. You've become Hard to Get.

Second, she may, indeed, not like you after your testing and disqualifying action. She may remain a bitch—of course, that is her right—but the difference will be how you feel about yourself.

BNBs often feel shame and humiliation after approaching a hot woman, because they've either groveled for her approval (ugh) or gotten mad and called her a bitch (double-ugh). When you perform a Hard to Get action, and she gets angry, **you** leave the interaction feeling good about yourself. You told the truth, and did it in a way that you can feel good about. Heck, other women will find that attractive in you, even if the woman you were talking to didn't.

COMMONLY VOICED RISK #3: "This may work for other men, but it wouldn't work for me because of [insert your reason]. Therefore testing and disqualifying is an unacceptable risk for me." This is the SNAVE syndrome all over again: "This will never work."

We'll let you in on a secret: You can always find a reason why the coaching you get "will never work." And too many BNB men spend their lives trying to prove to everyone around them that techniques that can work for everyone else would never work for them.

If you are one of those men, you must change. After many years of practice, your brain will keep telling you why nothing will ever work for you, even as you practice the techniques in this book. Your brain will keep telling you that "nothing will ever work," and it's not likely to stop.

But you do have the choice to ignore the "nothing will ever work" thoughts that your brain keeps generating. When those thoughts show up, don't argue. But don't believe those thoughts, either. And don't argue with us as you are reading this book. Just take some of the simple actions that we are teaching you in this book, and watch the results happen.

THE ECONOMY OF RISKS

BNB men either risk too much ("The woman at the coffee shop was nice to me, I'm going to stop all my other dating and concentrate on making things work with her") or risk too little ("I can't say 'hi' to a woman I like—what if it ruins her whole day?").

The man who risks too much always ends up rejected, used by women, and alone.

The man who doesn't risk enough always ends up alone, too, because no woman knows he's even interested.

The good news is there is a "middle way" to take risks with women. This way incorporates building trust by taking appropriate, step-by-step risks.

You see, trust is built when you allow a "give and take" with women. If you risk too much—and only give—then trust can't be built. Likewise, if you risk too little—and don't give anything—then the trusting interaction never even has a chance to start.

It's like when a business owner starts a new relationship with an untried, brand-new vendor. First, the business owner places a small order—in effect, taking a small risk on the unknown vendor. And in return, the vendor gives a small amount of product—in effect, building trust by giving something back, and giving a return on the business owner's risk.

When that transaction has worked, the business owner will increase the order, placing a larger one next time. And, in return, the vendor will give more back. And so it goes. Larger and larger orders are placed, with more and more trust building up between the parties involved.

The business owner wouldn't start by giving a $100,000 order to a new, untried vendor. It would be too risky. Likewise, if the business owner never places any order, nothing will ever happen.

We'll never forget one of our first clients—a sincere, intelligent young man who also happened to be a bit of a BNB. He was interested in his hairdresser, and finally got up the nerve to ask her out.

On the day of the date, he called her and left a message that he had rented a limo for their date and also a penthouse hotel room where they could have a secluded dinner. Shockingly for him—but not at all surprising to us—his date called to cancel the date a few hours later. "It just doesn't feel right," she told him.

It didn't feel right because he was taking far, far too much of a risk for a first date. And he freaked out his date by doing so.

We suggest you think about risks with a woman the same way the business owner thinks about money. You start by taking a small, penny ante risk—perhaps by saying hi. Then she risks back, by being nice, asking you a question, or showing her interest in you. Then you might move on to slightly larger risks. If those go well, you increase the risk level again, until you are up to much bigger risks—asking for her phone number, kissing her, and getting her somewhere private to get sexual.

We'll show you the Hard to Get risks you must take later in this book. But for now, start getting used to the idea that you will have to take some small risks in order to get what you want with women.

Taking Appropriate Risks Shows You Value Yourself

Here's something you must know:

A man who won't show that he values himself has <u>no value</u> to an attractive woman.

You may think it's unfair. You may cry and mope and get all upset about it. But it's true. A man who won't show that he values himself has no value to attractive women.

And the best way to show that you have value—and to value yourself—is to take a risk in how you behave, and to put making yourself happy ahead of making her happy.

That means testing, disqualifying, and having enough self-respect to risk being Hard to Get.

Now, some men believe that the best way to show hot women that you have value is to put down other men.

After all, it's often said that women want high-status men. This is true, but there are several routes to appearing "high-status."

Many men focus on the hardest ways to appear high-status—trying to one-up other men, or obsessing about being the alpha male.

We want to spend a few minutes talking about the alpha male concept right now, because it is so important and so widely misunderstood.

Let's start with this question: Have you ever seen a group of men competing for a woman's attention? Have you seen them all showing off, "cock-blocking" each other, and generally trying to be the biggest jerk around?

Have you perhaps even been a part of this competition?

Then have you ever seen a man who is **not** involved in the competition, who simply comes up to the woman, says a few words, and walks off with her?

We see it all the time. In fact, we, or our students, are often the ones walking off with the woman. That man who walked off with the woman was the alpha male.

The alpha male, in case you do not know, is the "top dog" in a dog pack (or the "top male animal" in any group of animals, like the "top monkey" in a monkey troop). He's the highest-status male around.

According to biologists, the alpha male gets "priority access to limited resources." That means he gets the best food and the hottest females. It's priority access. The other guys have to wait their turn in line… if they get a turn at all.

So here's what happens.

Men who want to succeed with women hear about this alpha male idea, and decide that they need to become more alpha. They figure that if they can just be the "top dog" among men, they'll be sufficiently high-status to get the women they desire. And they figure that the way to do this is to push around other men, act tough, and generally become a world-class jerk. They think a lot about "being alpha" and "appearing alpha." They worry about it. They argue about it on Internet discussion boards.

But it's all a trap, and we want to save you from it right now, once and for all.

You see, if you spend your time worrying about being alpha, trying to push other guys down, then you are **not** an alpha male.

There's an actual, scientific name for what you've become. That name is:

"Alpha wannabe."

And if you've fallen into the trap of becoming an alpha wannabe, you can be assured of one thing:

The **real** alpha males—the ones who **are** getting the women you desire—are **laughing** at you.

If you want to know **why** the real alpha males would laugh at your attempts to become alpha—and how the **real** "alpha men" get to the "top of the heap," and thus get the girls—then read on.

Here's the fact that real alpha me" don't want you to know: **Trying** to be the alpha male—that is, pushing other guys around, acting tough, and worrying a lot about how alpha you are—actually makes you **less** alpha.

That's right—being an "alpha wannabe" actually makes you **less** alpha, and **less** attractive.

This is an important point, and we want you to really get it, so let us put it another way, to make it absolutely clear:

When you worry about competing against other men—that is, obsessing about how alpha you are—you actually make yourself **less** alpha. You make yourself **lose** the competition.

But here's a strange truth.

The man who comes up "out of nowhere" and walks off with that hot woman, while everyone else is competing and showing off and trying to look tough, is **not** caught up in "trying to be alpha."

Because he's not part of the competition, he can simply concentrate on testing, disqualifying, and doing the other little-known Hard to Get actions we are revealing to you in this book.

He can bypass the other men who are caught up in the hopeless task of "out alpha-ing" each other.

It's a little bit like a fight scene in a kung fu movie.

Have you ever seen a kung fu movie where two gangs are fighting each other, but there's one guy standing off to the side, not participating? He's not caught up in competing with the other "alpha-wannabe" men. He's not trying to prove himself, or to show off. He's just standing there.

Then, near the end of the fight, he swoops in and makes one or two decisive moves that finish the fight.

That is the path of the true alpha male.

So here's what to do:

Don't worry about being the alpha male. (We guarantee that real alpha males are not worrying about it.) Stop worrying about competing against other men for status. It's a foolish way to go.

Spend your mental energy on something that really matters—on **how** you interact with women.

Real alpha men don't think about being alpha. They don't think much about competing with other men. True alpha men are not trying to prove themselves.

They are, quite simply, men who have done the work to be good at being Hard to Get. They have mastered a few fundamental skills so well that few men can "beat" them.

It's that simple.

CONCLUSION

What have we learned in this chapter?

We've seen that being Easy to Get—and trying to seduce **any** woman—does not work. The BNB tries for all women, and therefore gets no women, and ends up alone and ashamed.

Testing and disqualifying shows that you are a Hard to Get Man, and focuses you on the women who will be most attracted to you— which is often the most attractive women, who are used to men groveling for their attention.

But it's easy to mess it up. You must test and disqualify properly, or you are just an Impossible to Get Man and, once again, you will end up alone. But, unlike the Easy to Get BNB, who is alone and ashamed of himself, as an Impossible to Get Man, you'll be alone and angry and resentful. Not much of an improvement.

Testing and disqualifying women puts the seduction on your terms, focuses your attention on the women you can succeed with, makes you interesting and intriguing to those women, and starts the seduction process.

But testing and disqualifying means taking some risks. You need to start getting your head around the idea that, when you test or disqualify a woman, you might make her angry or upset her in some way. But remember, we also talked about how conflict, done properly, can be seductive to a woman, so you may find that a willingness to upset a woman, from time to time, actually works to your advantage.

We talked about how the economy of risks, used properly, will get you a lot farther with women than risking too much or too little. We talked about the importance of risking the appropriate amount, and gauging her response to your risk before you risk any more with her.

We talked about how taking Hard to Get actions shows a woman that you value yourself, and we talked about how a man who won't show that he values himself has **no value** to attractive women.

And we talked about how, if you want to be successful with women, you must abandon the idea of being the alpha male, and focus your attention on being a Hard to Get Man—no matter what other men around you are doing.

In the next chapter, we're going to reveal to you the single idea that is at the core of using Hard to Get actions to succeed in seduction—and the one new thing we've learned since writing *How to Succeed with Women* that has made seduction 80% easier for our students than it ever was before.

CHAPTER 3

Connecting and Disconnecting: Your Key to Easily and Quickly Becoming the Hard to Get Man That Hot Women Pursue

HOW YOU ARE HARD TO GET RIGHT NOW

Mike came to us with the same problem that a lot of men have.

See if you can relate to it yourself.

Mike said, "I'm able to get fat women, or women I'm not attracted to, to desire me—no problem. In fact, I can even get women that **other** men find attractive to like me... but I don't find them attractive at all! It's the women that **I** find attractive that I can't seem to get the time of day from, no matter what I do."

Does that sound familiar?

Are you good at "accidentally" seducing women you **aren't** attracted to?

Lots of men are.

We want to take a few moments to explore why that is. Because the answer to the question "Why can you seduce women you aren't attracted to?" is **central** to becoming a Hard to Get Man.

So how come you can seduce women you aren't attracted to, but not the ones you want?

The answer is simple—and we've hinted at it earlier in this book.

So here's why you are able to seduce women you **don't** desire: With women you **don't** desire, you are willing to both connect and **disconnect**.

And, by so doing, you become Hard to Get... and they pursue you.

Think about it.

With women you are **not** attracted to:

* **You don't avoid potential conflicts.** In fact, you are okay with having some conflict.

* **You don't care overmuch about what she thinks.** In fact, you want her to think that her thoughts are not your top priority.

* **You don't worry much about her feelings.** In fact, you want her to think that her feelings are not your top priority.

* **You think about what makes you feel good,** more than you think about what makes her feel good.

* **You don't worry** that she'll see something in you that might push her away. In fact, you may even **want** her to see such things.

* **You don't spend every moment of every interaction trying to connect with her.**

* **You are more honest about who you are** and what you want. You show yourself, "warts and all."

Important: These are **all** disconnecting actions, and they all make you Hard to Get.

And when you do them with women you don't desire, the women you don't desire want you.

But the corollary is also true: if you do these things with women you **do** desire, those women will want you, too.

We'll go into "why" in a moment. But first, we want to handle an objection you are probably already having.

As we discussed earlier, women who you don't like are more likely to like you because you naturally take Hard to Get actions with them. In response to this fact, there's a good chance that your brain started acting up. It probably started saying, "But no, that's not true! Hot women are less desperate than fat ones—and it's that desperation that makes the fat chicks like me, not any Hard to Get actions that I'm taking."

There is some truth in that objection—but, thankfully, there's less truth in it than you think.

You see, we've seen over and over again that a "loser" man can "accidentally" seduce a hot woman... provided that he himself does not think that she's hot.

David has a personal experience of this himself. He says:

"Years ago, when I didn't know anything about dating and seduction, there was a girl who worked in a local new-age bookstore that I became friends with.

"I didn't find her attractive, but a **lot** of men did. We'd go places and she'd be approached by guys, over and over and over. But I wasn't interested. I don't know why... I just didn't find her hot. And, perversely, as time went on she made it clearer and clearer that she wanted to have sex with me. Me—the one man who didn't seem to want her!

"We even went on a trip to California together, and slept in the same bed, and she kept coming on to me so much that I finally 'gave in' and had sex with her. And even though I was achieving what other men would have thought of as their sex life's ultimate dream, I was never that impressed by it... because, for whatever reason, I disagreed with most of the world, and didn't find her hot."

And it isn't just David who's experienced this. We've often been impressed by the beauty of some of the women that some of our students just aren't interested in.

The bottom line is this: Attraction is highly personal, no matter what you may think.

And here's something else interesting:

If you've ever "accidentally" seduced a woman you weren't interested in, then you have done disconnecting, and used Hard to Get actions.

You just need to understand what those Hard to Get actions are. Then you'll get a clear, exact sense of how to use them on purpose. You'll be able to do those actions with the women you **do** desire, rather than with the women that you **don't.**

THE LIMITATIONS OF CONNECTION IN SEDUCING WOMEN

You must be able to connect with women to seduce them, but as we said in Chapter 1, it's a mistake to **only** connect. And that is the mistake that most men make.

Understand this: Most men who are interested in hot women—you, and all of your competition, to be precise—make the same mistake. It's the mistake of the Easy to Get Man. After reading this book, you will never have to make that mistake again. Whew!

It's easy to fall into the "only try to connect with a woman" trap.

The (wrong) idea is this: Connect with a woman enough, on enough levels, and she'll want to have sex with you.

After all, creating a sufficient sense of connection with a woman often **does** work to get her in bed. We've had a lot of success that way, and so have our students.

And if you think about the best interactions you've had with women, they probably were interactions where you felt like you "totally connected." Naturally, you'll want to reproduce that connected sensation with any woman you are trying to seduce.

But once you have the tool of disconnection at your disposal, you'll be shocked by how much faster and easier your seductions of hot women are.

Think of it this way: Just for a second, imagine that you are a hot babe. MMMM! (Hey now, don't imagine it **that** much!) As a hot woman, men are always coming at you, trying to get your attention and your approval. Men are constantly performing as a way of trying to build a connection with you.

Men never disagree with you. Instead, they always tell you that you are right, that you are fascinating, that your opinions are unique and amazing, and that your outlook on the world is perfect. Oh, and that everything about you is beautiful, 100% of the time. You can behave any way you like, and act as mean and difficult as you want, and they never complain or confront you. They never say no to you, nor to any of your requests, no matter how outrageous those requests are. They do everything you say in the hopes of connecting with you further.

While this might be fun at first, imagine it going on for weeks, even **years**—every single day, practically everywhere you go.

You'd start to feel really crowded, with all these men trying to get "into your space" all the time. In fact, the psychological crowding of all these men trying to connect with you might actually get to be quite claustrophobic!

Now, on top of that feeling of men always coming at you, imagine how **boring** all these men would become. Their constant agreement, compliments, obedience, and absolute lack of challenge of any nature would, in time, become practically unendurable.

Welcome to the world of the hot woman. Even though she doesn't know it, she's begging for a man who can provide some challenge to her, who is interesting, and who, for once, is **not** crowding her with his constant need to connect with her.

She's waiting for a man who can disconnect, as well as connect with her.

She's waiting for a man who will treat her the way he treats a woman he's not attracted to.

To review: Men who are trying to always connect with women:

✱ Make women feel crowded by their constant need to connect.

✱ Bore women by their obedience to her every whim.

✱ Accept women's bad behavior without confrontation or accountability.

✱ Always agree with the woman so they'll seem "just alike."

✱ Always try to make the woman feel good.

✱ Put "getting along with the woman" above any other consideration.

And along the way, he makes the BNB mistakes of giving things he doesn't want to give, doing things he doesn't want to do, offering things he doesn't want to offer, and agreeing with things he doesn't agree with.

The Power of Disconnection in Attracting Women

"Disconnection" is the act of giving a woman something to "climb over" or to "get through" in order to get to you.

Let's look at a couple of real-world examples of how being willing to create disconnection can be attractive, even when there's a lot of competition:

First, consider this. Have you ever wondered why cats always seem to go to the person in the room who likes cats the least?

It's true. Put a cat in a roomful of people, and it will usually ignore the people who are saying, "Here kitty, kitty, kitty," or making kissy noises, or any of the other ridiculous things people do to get cats to approach them. Those people are all trying to create connection with the cat—which, for most cats, will push the cat away.

Then, as the cat lovers look on with dismay, the cat will go to the person who is least interested in cats, who doesn't like cats, or who is even allergic to cats.

That's because the one who's not a cat lover does things that create some **disconnection** between the cat and himself. He doesn't look directly at the cat, while everyone else is. He might move away physically, while everyone else is crowding forward. He doesn't reach out to the cat, as everyone else is constantly doing.

In this way he accidentally does Hard to Get, disconnecting actions. These disconnections create space for the cat to move into, rather than being the crowding, connecting actions that everyone else is using to push the cat away. His Hard to Get actions create a sense of intrigue. And the cat goes for it, and in no time is rubbing up against the one man who is Hard to Get, while all the cat lovers watch and cry.

Now, it's more complicated to do that with a hot woman, but the principle is the same, and you need to know it.

Here's another example. Have you ever wondered why gay men so often have hot women hopelessly in love with them? We've seen it many times. A super-hot babe who is always surrounded by hetero men, who would do anything for a crumb of her attention, will be forlornly attracted to a gay man who, by his very nature, will never have sex with her.

There are a number of reasons why this is so, but a big one is that the gay man constantly performs Hard to Get actions. He doesn't hold back on his opinions with her. He's not groveling or apologetic. He doesn't spend his every moment with her trying to establish the strongest connection possible. In fact, he's not afraid to disagree with her, criticize how she looks, or even piss her off.

And all that makes him ten times more interesting than the men who are always in her face trying to build connection with her. So she pursues him, even though it's hopeless, while all the groveling hetero men who are constantly trying to connect with her watch and cry.

HOW BNB'S DISCONNECT WITH WOMEN

We've probably convinced you of the importance of disconnecting with women to become Hard to Get. But most men—and especially BNBs—do disconnection all wrong. After spending so much groveling energy trying to connect with a hot woman, the BNB reaches his breaking point and finally does a disconnect—in the most unappealing way possible.

These "connection-only" men do sometimes disconnect from women they've been pursuing. But they do it in such a harsh way that it destroys any interest that the woman might have in him.

When BNBs disconnect with hot women, they do it harshly and completely anti-seductively, using the following mistaken tactics:

* **Angry Insults**. A BNB who has finally given up on connecting with a hot woman will sometimes get angry, yell, and call the woman a bitch or worse. We don't have to tell you that this form of disconnecting is not intriguing to a hot woman.

* **Taking Your Ball and Going Home.** Even more commonly, the BNB disconnects with a woman he's been pursuing by simply withdrawing entirely. He refuses to share the truth about what's going on with him and refuses to confront what is actually going on. He stays home and sulks by himself. If she does reach out to him at all, he's unresponsive.

* **Becoming a Whiney Baby.** When a BNB doesn't get the connection he wants with a woman, he'll also sometimes become a whiney baby, bombarding the woman with high-pitched complaints about how unfair it is that she doesn't want him, after everything he's done for her.

Actually, becoming a whiney baby is just a variation of becoming an angry insulter. As Stuart Smalley said, "Whining is anger forced through a very small opening." When you whine to a woman, you are just showing her another face of your anger. You are disconnecting, sure—but in a very permanent, unappealing way.

Because of his imbalance of connection and disconnection in the interaction, the BNB man ends up giving up on women he could have had sex with, simply because he connects too much at first, then disconnects too harshly when it's all over.

The bottom line is this: If you don't disconnect properly with women, you will always go to extremes. You will either:

Give your power to women

>   *OR*

Be super-pissed at them

Be a submissive puppy-dog

> *OR*

Be impossible to get

Grovel to women

> *OR*

Destroy all possibility of sex

"Suck up to women"

> *OR*

Try to be an alpha male

THE TWO KINDS OF DISCONNECTIONS YOU MUST KNOW TO GET WOMEN TO PURSUE YOU

We teach two kinds of disconnections in our programs: "truth" disconnects and "canned" disconnects. We'll go into great detail on these later in this book, but for now, let's give you an overview.

1) Truth disconnects. Here's something weird: Men go crazy trying to find the perfect way to disconnect seductively with women. They don't know what to do. But 99% of the time, the answer is often staring them in the face in the form of the behavior of the woman they are trying to seduce.

Put another way: Have you ever been treated shabbily by a woman you were trying to seduce? Has she ever been bitchy, moody, rude, angry, or difficult?

(Hint: The answer is, "Of course.")

You've probably wondered what to do when a woman does those things. And you've probably ended up just taking her bad behavior, or ignoring it, or making it into a joke and laughing it off.

And you certainly haven't gotten laid for all your efforts with her.

Well, it turns out that you can use these bad female behaviors as sources for perfect disconnections. You can turn the tables on her and her bad behavior, simply by properly pointing out the truth about what is actually going on.

A truth disconnect is a disconnection that you make with a woman by drawing attention to the truth about her mood, her behavior, or your experience of her.

And a woman provides an **abundance** of opportunities to disconnect with her by calling her attention to how she's behaving.

For instance, this happened at one of our Approach Camps: We were walking down a street in a bar area around midnight. We saw three girls together, and one of them looked really angry and upset.

David said "hi" to her, and she just grunted back. So David simply reflected back what was actually going on with a truth disconnect.

He said, "Wow, that's pretty rude. You look really angry."

She softened immediately. "Oh, I'm sorry," she said. "I've just been having a hard night."

David said, "Okay, but it's time to cheer up now. What bars have you been going to?"

And their conversation took off.

Please note: David didn't make a joke of her bad behavior. And he didn't get angry. He didn't pretend it didn't happen, and he didn't try to make things better. He didn't try to connect with her, thinking (wrongly) that connecting to an upset, angry woman is seductive (because it's not).

He simply drew her attention to how she was behaving—the one thing most men **won't** do with a bitchy, attractive woman—and he changed the entire dynamic of the situation. He taught her the proper way to treat him, and she had to "move toward him" energetically, changing her behavior to fit his desires.

And in that way, a good interaction—and, finally, a real connection—formed between them.

If you are one of those guys who objects to everything anyone tells you, then you are probably objecting to this right now. Your brain is probably saying something like, "Hey, won't she be totally pissed off at me, and leave entirely?"

We said it before, and we'll say it again so you can "get" it: Yes, sometimes that will happen. But consider what happened to one of our students, Brian.

Brian was in a bar and talking to a woman who was extremely beautiful, but incredibly stuck-up and rude. After a couple of minutes of talking to her and having her be so bitchy, he said, "Hey, you know what. You're a really rude woman, and I'm not going to talk to you anymore." He then turned on his heel and walked away.

If you are like most men who have never disconnected from a woman, then you probably think the interaction with her was over. Quite honestly, he did, too. But he felt good about himself, and was telling himself that that was enough.

But about a half-hour later, when Brian was getting ready to leave, that same girl came up to him. She told him she was sorry for being a bitch, and offered him her phone number.

Will this happen 100% of the time? Of course not. But being willing to disconnect will give you the same power over women that jerky men have: the ability to get past their bad behavior and to have success with them.

2) Canned disconnects. A "canned disconnect" is a disconnecting phrase that you've memorized and practiced (hopefully **out loud**) until you can say it no matter how scared or intimidated you are. You then deliver this "canned disconnect" to women who need it, and let it work its magic.

Here are some examples of "canned disconnects:"

"Didn't your mom teach you to have better manners?"

"I thought you were smart and interesting, but it looks like you're also really mean. My mistake."

"Did you do something really bad in a past life?"

"You don't get out much, do you?"

Later in this book we'll give you more "canned disconnects" than you could ever need, and show you how and when to use them to disconnect from a woman, and to make her move towards you.

As you get better at using both kinds of disconnects, you'll find that women—and especially attractive women, for whom a man who can disconnect is a rare and valuable thing—will be more attracted to you and will pursue you in your interactions.

What Disconnecting Does

A properly executed disconnect with a woman makes you a Hard to Get Man.

1) Disconnection makes her take action. Specifically, disconnection creates in her a need to do one of two things:

First, to pursue you. When you disconnect properly from a woman, you become a commodity that she wants to pursue. You become the one man who isn't always groveling for her attention, but who also isn't harshly disconnecting and pushing her away forever. You are creating a distance between you, but it's a distance that she can bridge with you. Thus, you become interesting to her.

If you've done a truth disconnect, and busted her on her bad behavior, she may explain herself or even apologize.

Because she's rarely seen a man who was honest about having a negative judgment about her but who also wasn't being a total asshole at the same time, she'll feel compelled to reverse your negative judgment of her.

And because you've become an interesting, rare commodity, she'll want to hold your interest. She'll even try to entertain you, or prove herself to you. These are attempts on her part to come closer to you, because you have moved farther from her, and given her some space.

Or, second, she'll need to get rid of you. Yes, sometimes creating some space with a woman by doing a disconnect will end things with her entirely. It's a harsh reality. You'll have found out that she was a "no way," and thus you won't waste your time, money, or self-esteem on her.

You **want** one of these two things to happen. You **want** her to either try to come and get you, or to get rid of you entirely.

2) Disconnection shows you are a strong, bold, interesting man. Simply disconnecting with a woman harshly (by yelling at her, or by "taking your ball and going home") does not make you interesting, but a competent disconnection most definitely does.

3) Disconnection creates controversy. When you are connecting with a woman, you want to get along with her. And while proper connecting is important, it's likely that you've overdeveloped your connecting skills and underdeveloped your disconnecting skills.

It's different when you are disconnecting with a woman. When you are disconnecting, you want to create some controversy, because controversy is inherently interesting.

4) Disconnection gives her room to move toward you. If you want to have chemistry with a woman, you **both** must have room to move toward each other. If you don't give her room to move toward you, you won't have chemistry, and you'll rarely get success.

Think of it this way: **If you fulfill all of a woman's desires, she has no place to go but away.** She won't be able to move toward you because you are so busy moving toward her. Disconnection gives her a desire for **you** that is unfulfilled, and draws her in your direction. True disconnections demonstrate a difference between you and her and motivate her to work for your approval.

5) Disconnecting breaks your trance about her being hot and beautiful. When a man is entranced by a hot woman's amazing body, he naturally doesn't want to take any risks that might push her—and those amazing tits of hers—away.

When you do a disconnect, you take that risk, and thus break your trance about her beauty. And after you've successfully seduced a few women using disconnects—and seen how easily and well it works— you won't get as easily entranced by a woman's beauty again.

6) Disconnection gives her a reason to pursue you. When you are a Hard to Get Man, you are not a BNB. You are not a jerk. You are not meek, and you are not just a supplicant to her, hoping that she'll give you some crumb of attention. You are interesting!

Being able to connect and disconnect is an important part of what we are going to talk about next: having a Hard to Get Personality.

CONSTRUCTING A "HARD TO GET" PERSONALITY

A Hard to Get Personality is paradoxical. This means that a Hard to Get Man is not stuck on being just one way. He's not trying to be consistent.

Sometimes he's calming. Other times he's upsetting.

Sometimes he's predictable. Other times he's unpredictable.

Sometimes he's comforting. Other times he's not comforting.

Sometimes he's gentle. Other times he's fierce.

Sometimes he's excited. Other times he's placid.

Sometimes he agrees. Other times he disagrees.

Sometimes he's easygoing. Other times he's challenging.

Sometimes he's happy. Other times he's sad.

Sometimes he's tough. Other times he's loving.

Sometimes he's romantic. Other times he's "down-and-dirty" sexual.

As the poet Walt Whitman said, "I contradict myself, I contradict myself." The man with the Hard to Get personality has many different approaches to the world, which sometimes seem to contradict each other. That doesn't mean he's a liar. Instead, it means that there are many facets to his personality, and he's not afraid to express a wide variety of them.

CONTRAST: THE KEY TO THE HARD TO GET PERSONALITY

The odds are that when you are with a woman you are attracted to, you try to contrast with her as little as possible. You want to get along with her, so you repress your differences and focus only on your similarities.

This is a gigantic mistake. Remember, plenty of men have "friendships" with hot women, where they don't contrast, don't disagree, and always get along. Sadly for these men, they also get to listen as their hot women "friends" talk about having hot sex with the "jerks" (whom they don't always get along with).

If you want women you desire to pursue you, then you **must** develop your Hard to Get personality by improving your ability to contrast with a woman.

But first, a warning: You may also have heard people talk about the so-called seductive power of "matching and mirroring" with a woman.

"Matching and mirroring" is based on the idea that people like people who are like themselves. If you follow this theory, you try to be like her: If she leans back, you lean back. If she smiles, you smile. If she scratches her head, you scratch your head (not hers!). The idea of "matching and mirroring" is that if you can make your movements to be like hers, she will be comfortable with you and thus will like you.

The problem is this: **A woman being comfortable with you and liking you is not the same as her being attracted to you.** Matching and mirroring is not the key to seduction, because **difference is more attractive than sameness.**

Consider this truth: **Women like men who are like them, but when they want adventure, excitement, and intrigue, they look**

for men who are different from themselves. If you want to be seductive, that **different** man has to be **you.**

Between men and women, contrast is intriguing, attractive, and arousing. Sameness may sometimes get you laid, but it should **not** be the only tool you have in your seduction toolbox.

And here's another important point: While being "just like" a woman is not seductive in itself, neither is it seductive to have a woman agree with you all the time. If you can't contrast, if you can't agree **and** disagree, you are not creating any contrast between yourself and the woman. And that will make seducing her that much harder.

Here's the bottom line you need to know:

Agreement by itself is not seductive.

Disagreement by itself is not seductive.

The man with the Hard to Get, paradoxical personality does both. And he **is** seductive to women.

Here's a list of the personality traits of the Hard to Get, paradoxical personality. As you read this list, notice how each of these traits can create contrast if you express them with a woman.

TWO WAYS TO START PRACTICING
BEING CONTROVERSIAL WITH WOMEN:

1) Do a truth disconnect. Next time a woman is behaving badly, feed her behavior back to her. Don't make it an attack, simply say, "Wow, that was really rude. You're a really rude woman." This will open the door either to her apologizing or to a brief conflict. Remember the principles from this section: don't apologize and don't attack her, and see what happens.

2) Do a canned disconnect. Flip through this book and find the lists of disconnects, and try one out on a difficult woman. It will also either soften her or open up a small level of conflict. Either result is good.

We know it can be scary at first to do these disconnections with women and risk conflicts, even seductive conflicts. But will it really be more difficult and painful than what you are probably doing now—only trying to connect with women, putting up with crap from women, and only having conflicts with women where the entire interaction gets destroyed?

So start slowly and start small. Don't worry what happens. You'll start to develop yourself as a Hard to Get Man. And you'll become more and more attractive to women who, at this moment, may seem completely out of your reach.

CHAPTER 4

Light Disconnections

Special Note: *The next three chapters—chapters 4, 5, and 6—will give you every tool you'll ever need to get women to pursue you by being "Hard to Get."*

Because these chapters cover many, many possible circumstances, as you read them you may find yourself getting overwhelmed with all the options and possibilities.

Don't worry.

Chapter 7, "Putting It All Together," contains detailed examples and exact, "step-by-step" instructions of what to do and what to say both day-approach and night-approach settings.

By the end of this book you'll have an abundance of tools you can explore for years to come as you get hot women to approach you by being Hard to Get. These are in chapters 4, 5, and 6.

You'll also have a "by-the-numbers" system you can use, starting today. That's in chapter 7.

So relax, open your mind, and let's get started with "Light Disconnectors."

In this chapter we will teach you the **light disconnectors.** In later chapters we'll discuss medium and heavy disconnectors. We will show how and when to use them. This chapter will give you a surplus of tools that you can use in all situations with women. But first, we want you to know the basics of rewarding and punishing women.

REWARD AND PUNISHMENT

One of the key skills of being a Hard to Get Man is having the ability to both reward and punish women. In fact, a Hard to Get Man constantly rewards and punishes women. The Hard to Get Man is flexible in his approach with women and is constantly rewarding women when they are treating him well. He is generous with his rewards and enjoys the reward process. The Hard to Get Man also does not hesitate to punish a woman when she is nasty or mean. He goes in and holds his ground.

The BNB, on the other hand, is unable or refuses to reward and punish women. The BNB avoids anything emotional, intense, or risky. He prefers to stay safe and boring rather than take any risk at all. The Easy to Get Man rewards women all the time, even when they don't deserve it. The Impossible to Get Man punishes women without enough provocation. So reward and punishment can be a tricky process.

The Bad Boy Credo

You know who has massive flexibility with their behavior, specifically in their ability to reward and punish women? Bad boys. **Bad boys are constantly giving out rewards and punishments. You might even say that bad boys are Hard to Get.**

HOW TO REWARD WOMEN

By suggesting that you reward a woman, we mean that you should acknowledge her for doing something you like. Examples are if she says something interesting, does something sexy, says something funny, leans into you, etc. A reward lets her know she did something good, something you liked. A reward affirms behavior where she puts energy into the conversation and moves toward you. Rewarding a woman is about letting her know you enjoy your time with her and the interaction. Think of rewards as little nuggets of "good feelings" that are passed back and forth between the two of you.

In a typical conversation, you can reward women in various ways. We are going to touch on a few situations to give you an idea how to do it. We cover this topic in much greater depth in the Advanced Course.

The 4 levels of rewarding women are body language, attention, compliments, and time.

As you're getting to know a woman, do **not** sit on the edge of your seat totally focused on her like her little puppy dog. She must earn your full attention. If you're a typical BNB, you probably don't believe that a woman must **earn** your attention. So pay attention to this point: She must **earn** your full attention.

A woman earns your full attention as she gives you HER full attention. If she is talking on her cell phone or looking around the room instead of being focused on you, do not reward her, punish her instead (we'll talk about this in a minute).

Think about it this way: When you're with a woman, you should both be putting in equal amounts of energy. You are not just performing for her and doing all the work, and neither is she. The exchange of energy should be pretty equal. When it's not equal, you can bet that there is a problem.

The first level of rewards is the level of Attentive Body Language Rewards. This means you lean your body into hers and put out attentive body language, demonstrating that you're interested in what she is saying and that you're paying attention to her.

The second level of rewards is the level of the Simple Compliment Reward. These sorts of rewards are based on details of her attire, what she is talking about, or what she is saying. Here are some examples:

"I really like that scarf, it's beautiful."

"That's a really interesting point you just made."

"It's so cool that you're interested in PETA."

We always recommend you give authentic rewards to women, not superficial bullshit rewards. If you give a woman insincere compliments or rewards she will likely spot it and think you're a player, a liar, and someone she wants to get away from. If you want to be a Hard to Get Man, one of the practices you must put in place is to **be authentic** when you're with women. Be authentic in your rewards and punishments.

The third level of rewards is the level of Intimate Rewards. These sorts of rewards are deeply emotional and personal. You compliment her on details about her personality, essential character, and/or the type of person she is.

For example:

"You're a really deep person. I like that about you."

"You have such a great sense of humor."

"You are so fun to be with."

"You have an amazing mind."

"You are really insightful."

"You have a really fun spirit."

"You have a great sense of detail."

The fourth level of rewards is the level of the Time Rewards. Applying time rewards means you are rewarding her by sharing your desire to spend more time with her. In a bar situation this equates to taking her to another club or venue. When you meet a woman at a niche event, a time reward means asking for her phone number or asking her out on another date. All time rewards involve you expressing an interest to spend more time with her.

PUNISHING WOMEN 101

We know that you are probably much better at complimenting and rewarding women than you are at punishing them. Most likely you're a guy who doesn't punish women, and constantly sells out with women. We're going to change that right now. So pay attention.

When you punish a woman, you tease her, insult her, challenge her, or actively show disinterest in her. You punish women at peak moments during a date when you feel she is being disrespectful, bitchy, patronizing, rude, or not paying attention to you when you are talking.

Think about punishment this way: You need to be a man of high value. High-value people do not take shit and yet do not feel the need to prove themselves. So, you in essence bust a woman for her bad behavior. You do not let her get away with shit. Do not feel obligated to take her shit, nor do you waste your time with a woman who is being rude to you.

Nice guys tend to reward women, even when women do not deserve it. Nice guys then start to feel resentful. They bottle up their anger until they explode and punish brutally. Does that ring true for you? Do you know anyone who does that with women? Do you know guys who act nice to women and do things they don't want to do and then occasionally get really angry and scream, yell, and pout?

Going ballistic on women is not how you punish women. Acting crazy or cruel is what the immature crying bitch does when he doesn't get his way. What we're talking about is not stifling your disagreements with women, not avoiding conflict, and not squashing your opinions or views.

We are talking about busting women on their bad behavior. You highlight their bad behavior; you don't suppress it. Being up-front with the things that bother you is where it's at. Your job is to assert yourself around women and let them know when they've crossed the line.

The first form of punishment is Punishment through Withdrawal of Attention. When a woman shows a lack of enthusiasm or interest in you when you are talking to her, one easy form of punishment is to look at your watch, look around the bar, go to the bathroom, take a cell call, etc. You are punishing her by not paying attention.

The next form of punishment is Punishment through Comment. 99.9% of guys do not bust women on their bad behavior. Most guys ignore bad behavior, and yet inside they disconnect and plan to never talk to the woman again because they are afraid of conflict. Women are hungry for guys to stand up for themselves and have self-respect. Women want guys to stand up to them without becoming psycho angry guys. So practice stating the truth in a matter-of-fact way and you'll be in the game.

The point of all punishments is that you are bringing to light a woman's nasty behavior and showing her you don't like it.

You might say things like:

"You're not very nice to strangers."

"You are one of those women who meets a guy and has to take a cell call every five minutes."

"You need an attitude adjustment."

"Didn't your mom teach you to have better manners?"

"I thought you were smart and interesting, but it looks like you're also really mean. My mistake."

"Hey little girl, get with the program."

The ultimate form of punishment: Withdrawal of attention all together. The ultimate way of punishing a woman is to simply walk away and not talk to her anymore. If a woman is just mean-spirited and terrible to be around, just get the hell out of there and stop talking to her. That's it. Simple.

Women often test men to see how they respond to anger and other intense emotions. Does the guy flip out and run away? She then thinks he's a wimp. Does he fight back in an abusive manner? He is gone because he is not trustworthy. If you can hold your ground with women when they attack you without becoming an apologetic wimp, and still not become an abusive asshole, they will respect you and likely will want to spend more time with you. Men who can hold their ground in the way we are talking about are indeed Hard to Get Men.

Remember, emotion is good. Extreme emotion is even better. Women thrive in situations that are highly emotional. So, when a woman gets extremely angry, happy, or sad she's engaged. One of the reasons BNBs are so boring is that they avoid emotions. Therefore, pushing up intense emotions with women is good. You might not be comfortable with a woman getting upset with you and "losing it." But trust us when we tell you that if you are able to ride the wave of intense emotions with women, sex is often on the other side and/or a deeper connection.

Think about it this way: **for a woman to jump from bored to horny is pretty far, but for her to go from anger to horny is a much shorter jump.** Therefore, pushing a woman until she has an intense emotional reaction is not a bad thing. It can be a good thing. But it is risky.

DISCONNECTORS

When you use disconnectors, you are being authentic with women yet challenging them by asking questions that demonstrate your powerful personality. You are showing that you don't care what they think about you. You are showing women that you are different than they are and that difference is cool. You are actually sharing about yourself and your uniqueness and allowing them the same opportunity to share with you about their unique personality.

The Disconnection Spectrum: from Light to Heavy

There is a spectrum of techniques for disconnecting with women. On one end of the spectrum you have light disconnection, where you share your opinions, thoughts, and feelings in a way that risks offending her or turning her off. On the other end of the spectrum are heavy disconnectors that actively tease a woman, give her shit, and "bust" her. Our goal is that you understand the various forms of disconnection and have flexibility in your behavior with women. When you have flexibility you can then decide what a particular situation warrants and disconnect in the amount required.

Disconnection through Body Language

No matter where you are on the disconnection spectrum, managing your body language is a fundamental skill. To succeed with women you must understand how to convey interest and disinterest through your body language. Just as you can learn any skill, you **can** learn how to master your body language. The cool thing about body language is that when you use strong body language you also internally feel stronger and more confident.

Disinterested body language demonstrates to a woman that you are not looking for her approval or trying to impress or placate her. Disinterested body language makes her work to get your attention.

Disinterested Body Language Basics

Your first lesson in body language is to learn how to convey disinterest in a woman. Think about it this way. If you are a BNB and you are begging a woman to like you and be your friend, what do you do? You would most likely lean into her space, smile, and try to "give" as much energy as you could to her. But that's exactly the **wrong** approach. The Hard to Get Man knows that he needs to start an interaction with a woman by **not** giving too much and making a woman **earn** his full attention. This means you **lean back when you first meet a woman and while you are talking with her**. You don't appear overly available. You even let yourself appear to be disinterested and distracted and only give her little nuggets of attention.

Other Body Language Suggestions:

❋   Use strong eye contact. Make her look away before you do.

❋   Slow down your walk and manner.

❋   Allow yourself to take up space.

Why are we telling you to do these things? Because they send a signal to a woman that you are **not** needy. That you are not like all other guys begging for her attention. Through your body language you show a woman that you are not like guys who act like supplicating puppy dogs. You are different. You are sexy.

FALSE TIME CONSTRAINTS

Another basic skill that you can use at any stage of a seduction are false time constraints. We first developed the idea of false time constraints over ten years ago when we were writing *How to Succeed with Women*. Back when we were researching that book, we noticed that women responded more favorably if we were less available, if they knew an interaction was short, and if the interaction had a definite ending point. We also noticed that when we first approached a woman, the first question in her mind seemed to be, "How long is this guy going to talk to me and what does he want?" By using a false time constraint she knows you're not going to sit and talk to her forever when she most likely wants you to go away.

More importantly, a false time constraint tells her that you are not a needy BNB who wants to suck up all her time and energy. Just watch what most guys do when they approach a woman. They overstay their welcome and get nowhere. But you are different. By using false time constraints you demonstrate to a woman that you are not needy and not too available. You use the principle of scarcity to disconnect with her. Remember, the BNB is always available and has all the time in the world for a woman. The Hard to Get Man only has a limited amount of time, and he's not willing to wait around while a woman wastes his time.

So what exactly is a false time constraint? It's when you create a scarcity of you, thus becoming more valuable. You do so by offering only a little time to the woman. You are offering her only a little time to get to know you, talk to you, etc.

Here are a few examples of ways to introduce false time constraints into a conversation:

"I only have only minute, but..."

"I'm with my friends, I can only stay a few seconds, so..."

"I need to get going now. Write your phone number down right here
for later."

"I'm really busy but..."

"I am about to take off, if you want to get together you better say so right now or we'll likely never see each other again."

"If I didn't have to split right now, I'd stay around and make out with you, but I gotta go. "

Here is how you integrate false time constraints into an interaction with a woman:

* Stop an interaction early, thus leaving a woman wanting more.
* Don't be too available when setting up a date.
* Be the first to end an interaction or date.
* End on a high note during an interaction or date.
* End an interaction suddenly.
* Stop while it's still fun.
* Be honest with yourself, if you feel like stopping an interaction stop. Don't feel compelled to talk longer or hang out longer than you want.

LIGHT DISCONNECTION

As we mentioned earlier, disconnectors occur on a spectrum from light to heavy. We are going to start off easy with the light disconnectors. These are important because they demonstrate to a woman your personality and the ways in which you are different from her.

One way to think about light disconnectors is that you are bringing out yourself in a conversation. You say, do, and become things that a woman might dislike. We suggest you master these disconnectors and use them with women all the time. Light disconnectors also work in relating to guy friends as well. You are developing a stronger sense of "yourself" and mastering how to express yourself at all times and risk turning off others.

TOOL#1: QUESTIONS

A. Clarification Questions

Clarification questions are questions you ask where you seek to understand what someone is saying or meaning. Obviously these are not shocking or outrageous questions (we will get to those later). But keep in mind that BNBs never ask questions at all. They never risk showing that they do not understand someone or something.

When you ask someone to clarify a point they have made, you turn the tables on the interaction and make them answer to you. In business negotiations it's known that the person asking the questions is the one in control. Another good thing about clarification questions is that you get to see a woman's personality when she answers a clarification question. You see if she is open, bitchy, nasty, or what.

Examples of clarification questions:

"What do you mean by [x]?"

"I don't understand you."

"Could you explain that further?"

"Teach me. I'm your student, I know nothing…"

"Can you give me an example of what you mean?"

"I'm confused. Say that again."

"What do you think the causes of [x] are?"

B. Stealth Disconnector Questions

These sorts of disconnectors seem like connectors, but in fact you are in truth disconnecting from a woman. These sorts of questions imply a difference in your perspective versus her perspective. At the same time these types of questions are not forceful enough to push her away. These sorts of questions are very useful when you are first getting to know a woman because they will draw her out and create a deeper conversation. However, these are not passive, wimpy questions. You might push her away and you might upset her.

Examples:

"You seem to be assuming..."

"Isn't there another way to see that?"

"What would be another way of seeing that?"

"Here's another point of view..."

"How do you know that?"

"How did you form that point of view?"

"Why do you say that?"

"Can you expand on that some more?"

"Are you sure?"

"Where did you get this idea?"

"How can you verify that assumption?"

"What if you're wrong about [x]?"

"Do your friends and family feel the same way?"

"What are you implying?"

"That's a nice theory, but how does that apply to your actual life?"

TOOL #2: PLAYFUL AND SILLY DISCONNECTORS

A. Silly Compliments

Hot chicks have guys come up to them all the time like puppy dogs offering compliments such as, "You are so beautiful." Or, "I had to say hi to you because you are so attractive." These compliments are **boring** and **predictable**. And they imply a power differential between the man and the woman. The man puts himself in a lower power position and the woman is therefore in a higher power position. We say, "Screw that!" Do something that will break the ice differently. Compliment women the way a Hard to Get Man does, using a silly compliment.

You use Silly Compliments to show her you are silly, playful, and fun. Do you think BNBs use silly compliments? No way. They are so caught up in trying to come across as perfect and slick that they never risk coming across as silly or immature.

Silly compliments act as a disconnector because you put a woman on the defensive when you use them. She has to react. She can either tease you back, thus playing along somehow, or she will ignore you. Sometimes a woman will even get upset and give you the evil eye. Whatever her response, you know right away if this woman is worth playing with or not.

Here are some examples:

"You're really fun for a nut."

"You'd be sexy as a Martian girl."

"You're feisty. I like that."

"It's fun to meet an aggressive woman." (Say this when a woman is being very passive.)

"You're really beautiful." (Say this in a funny voice.)

"I like you, are you sure you're a woman and not a man?"

"You've got beautiful eyes. Are you wearing colored contacts?

"You are a really loud dresser. I like that."

"You seem really nice. Probably too nice for me."

"You are silly. Silly like a teenage girl when she has a crush on a boy."

B. Ways to Act Silly and Playful

Along with asking silly questions, you can also use silly body language and do silly things. Here are a few examples:

Stick your tongue out at her and make a funny face.

Stare at her cross-eyed.

Throw something at her like a napkin or a penny.

Shake salt or pepper on her arm.

Throw an ice cube at her.

C. Asking Wacko Questions

Another way to joke around with women is to ask wacko questions. These sorts of questions work best in a bar situation. The entire point of these sorts of questions is to put a woman on the defensive and get her to play with you. We recommend asking wacko questions in conjunction with more serious questions as a way to loosen up a woman and let her know you can be playful and silly. When you are playful and silly, you are in the perfect mode to attract women. Women love to be around fun guys because they are not boring.

Some examples:

"Hey, do you believe in ESP?"

"Have you ever put a hex on a guy when you were really mad?"

"Do you think things happen for a reason?"

"Do you believe in vampires?"

"Do you think vampires are sexy?"

"Have you ever been abducted by aliens?"

"Would you have sex with a ghost?"

"Are you into witchcraft?"

"Have you ever participated in a séance?"

"Do you know any friends who are interested in the occult?"

"What's the craziest thing a guy has said to you?"

"Do you know anyone who has been abducted by a UFO?"

D. Stealth Disconnector: Shocking, Surprising Questions

The Hard to Get Man makes strong statements when he communicates with women. Therefore, the Hard to Get Man pushes himself to take larger risks with women and therefore asks shocking and surprising questions. By asking these questions you are showing her that you don't care if she likes you or not. Nor are you the sort of guy that is trying to play it safe by asking predictable and boring questions.

Here's the deal. These questions are designed for bars, clubs, and other places where chicks are drinking. They aren't going to fly in a quiet bookstore.

Another tip: These questions are probably not going to be the best things to ask right out of the gate. In other words, approach a woman with a different opener and then a while later throw one of these stealth disconnectors into the conversation.

Examples:

"What would you do if you had a penis for a day?"

"Which of your girlfriends would you most want to kiss and why?"

"What was the worst part of your day?"

"Would you rather have ADD or OCD?"

"What would you do if you could be invisible for a day?"

"What is the oddest dream you've had recently?"

"Why do you suppose we have five fingers?"

"If you had to lose your eyesight or your hearing, which one would you choose to lose and why?"

"This place sucks. Don't you think?"

"I'm bored, what about you?"

"If you had to go to prison for committing one crime, what crime would you commit?"

"If you were a boy, what would your parents have named you?"

E. Light Teasing

One of the best ways to disconnect from women is to tease them. Teasing is an entire art in itself. We could do an entire book just on teasing women, but we'll save that for another time.

Teasing women is flirty, fun, and can be exciting and sexy. Remember back in Chapter 1 when we discussed qualities of the Hard to Get Model? When you tease women, you demonstrate a few of these qualities and show that you are unpredictable and hard to figure out, that you are fun and exciting, that you have confidence in yourself, and that you're not afraid of conflict.

Examples:

"You're the kind of person who..." (You could say that she is a brat, is mean, is weird, is nasty to strangers, is moody, etc.)

"Is there something seriously wrong with you?"

"I have a bad feeling about you."

"You look really dangerous."

"What was it like to be in prison?"

"What a great stripper outfit."

"How long were you a crackhead?"

"You're really NICE, too nice."

"You're fun to be around, like a teenage girl."

"You look innocent, but something tells me that's not true."

"Did you do something really bad in a past life?"

"You don't get out much, do you?"

F. Give Her Nicknames or Pet Names

Most guys think you can only give women pet names once you are in a relationship, but we disagree. One of the ways you can greatly speed up a connection with a woman and increase the sex vibe is to use pet names. By using a pet name and repeating it on and off throughout a conversation it becomes a way of making a deeper connection.

This is how you use a pet name. A few minutes into a conversation you say to a woman, "Your new name is Shorty." You then start calling her a pet name like "Shorty" every few minutes while you talk to her. You create an odd bond between the two of you makes her feel more comfortable talking to you and therefore more trust and connection with you.

Examples of Pet Names:

The Nut

Muffin

Spanky

Kiddo   Baby Cakes   Space Case

Little Girl   Dork

Shorty   Weirdo

Doofus   My Little Bad Girl

Cutie Pie   Oddball

CONCLUSION

These Light Disconnectors are great early on in interactions, and when the woman may need a little "correction" but she doesn't need to put "back in line" in any major way.

As you deepen your interaction with a woman, you'll move on to using some Medium Disconnectors. Read on to find out all about them!

CHAPTER 5

Medium Disconnectors

We are now onto the medium level of disconnectors. These disconnectors are more risky and require you to bring out more of yourself in the interactions with women.

Medium disconnectors are about being fun, playful, silly, and outrageous. They are also about you revealing more of your personality and being more ballsy.

With medium disconnectors, you are also stepping more into the area of PUNISHING women. We spoke earlier about how you need to know when to reward a woman for her good behavior and then also punish a woman when she is rude or mean to you. Whenever a woman is mean or nasty to you, medium and heavy disconnectors work well in letting a woman know she has insulted you.

Medium disconnectors are more for bar environments than for day approaches (You'll see full examples of each in Chapter 7). You don't want to just tease a woman and not do anything else to make her feel connected to you. You need to combine teasing a woman with other questions. You will also need to tease her and reveal things about yourself if you expect her to feel connected to you.

We recommend teasing for a while and then switching topics to talk about more serious and intimate things for a while. Then again tease her for a while and move back to more serious topics. By flipping back and forth with topics, you create a type of flirty tension that tends to be appealing and attractive to women.

That said, here are some techniques to try.

TOOL #3: TRUTH DISCONNECTORS

A. Stating Her Obvious Emotions

As we've said before, one way to disconnect with women is to state their obvious emotions. We really want to pound this idea into you, so we'll say it again: When you tell a woman what her vibe is, you really make a strong statement. You demonstrate that you pay attention to details, that you are emotionally sensitive, and that you can talk about vulnerable subjects. You also show her that you don't hold back and talk about superficial bullshit. You pay attention to her emotions and then feed them back to her.

This isn't about being an asshole and trying to be mean to women. This is about giving a woman feedback on the emotions she is expressing. You can use this tool to tease a woman and give her shit about the vibes she is giving off. You can also do it in a serious way and generate a serious and contemplative conversation.

Stating a woman's emotions puts her in a defensive position, because by bringing to her attention that she seems preoccupied or distant, she either has to agree with you or disagree, therefore explaining herself to you. In either case you've engaged her on a deep level.

Stating a woman's emotions is risky business, though. You risk pissing a woman off when you tell her that, for example, she looks angry. She might say, "Yeah, I am angry. Go the fuck away." At the same time, by taking such risks with women you also open the door to an intimate and deep conversation that can easily lead to an extensive conversation, a date, a sex vibe, and more.

Stating a woman's obvious emotions can be used in day approaches when you see a woman in a coffee shop, but it also works well in bar situations. Stating a woman's obvious emotions will generate some interesting conversations, to say the least, and we highly recommend you experiment with this technique immediately.

Here are some examples:

"You look angry."

"You look like you're having a bad day."

"You look distraught."

"You seem really goofy."

"You seem really nervous in social situations."

"You look bitter."

"Life hasn't treated you very well, huh?"

"You look great tonight, but there is something off about you."

"You seem friendly but there is a bitter edge to you."

"You look really preoccupied."

"You are really boring."

"You look really aloof."

"You look like you're having a really bad day."

"You seem like you're having a hard time concentrating."

"You seem really nervous."

B. Make Her the Butt of Your Jokes

Yes, we are getting into scary territory here. One way to push disconnect with a woman you are talking to you in a bar-like environment is to tease her and make her the butt of your jokes. This will **definitely** get a reaction from her and make her respond. She might get angry, but you'll get her to respond.

Hot women, as we've said before, are treated like royalty. They are used to men acting like supplicating puppy dogs around them. Men run around buying hot women drinks, gifts, entry fees into clubs, and much more. Hot women are not, however, used to men teasing them and making fun of them. Hot women are used to belittling men, not becoming the butt of someone's jokes. So, this sort of teasing is a good thing to practice. You will quickly get a response and that's a good thing. Again, use this at a bar, or in a party-like atmosphere. It will certainly either have her come to you or move away.

Examples of making a woman the butt of your jokes:

Make blonde jokes. (Use any you know on a blonde woman.)

"You really do not have much of a sense of humor, do you?"

"Are you even worth it?"

"You are awfully moody. Do people tell you that often?"

"Is that something women tend to do?"

"Are you always such a psycho?"

"You really are high maintenance, aren't you?"

"You really are a drama queen aren't you?"

"You drama school dropout!"

"You must be the smart one around here."

"Just because you're used to being treated as a sex object doesn't mean I want to be."

"You are awfully serious, aren't you?"

C. Find Her Insecurities and Sensitive Topics

Another form of making a woman the butt of your jokes is to point out potentially sensitive things about her. Ditto on what we said about most men sucking up to hot women and not teasing them. Finding a woman's insecurities is an even more personal form of teasing a woman and making her the butt of your jokes. Therefore it's even more risky than the previous technique.

For you to find a woman's insecurities and tease her about them, you must point out **real** things. You cannot use stock or canned insults. You need to find things a woman is really sensitive about and bust her on those points.

Again, you are putting out that you have an edge and are a risk taker. You are also pushing her to have a conflict with you. The thinking behind this is that the conflict will either have a playful resolution and she will be more curious about you, or she will just think you are a jerk. In other words, **when you find a woman's** insecurities you might have to duck a punch or move your head to avoid being slapped.

Examples:

"Your ears are awfully big."

"Did you recently have a nose job?"

"Did you know that you have really bad posture?"

"You really need a makeover."

"What's up with the nervous tic?"

"What's up with the hairstyle?"

"You're sweating, are you nervous?"

"Why don't you smile, do you have bad teeth?"

"I can tell you are someone who holds back a lot in life."

"How long have you been single?"

"You look really tired. Are you a workaholic?"

"There are two types of people in this world: players and observers. I bet you're [pick one]."

"You talk a big game, but you just seem so insecure."

"Do you talk a lot when you're nervous?"

"You were sort of unpopular in high school, right? How did I know that?"

"Behind all the aloofness is a really sensitive and scared girl inside you."

D. Disqualifiers

A truly Hard to Get Man makes women work to get to know him. A Hard to Get Man, in fact, gives women obstacles to overcome to get to know him. He makes women come toward him by moving away from them.

We know that this is counterintuitive. We know that most guys pursue women and are used to jumping through hoops to get a woman. But you need to do things differently if you want to get different results. By making disqualifying statements you make a woman justify herself to you. Again, for these to be effective you cannot completely alienate her by being mean. You need to disqualify and then later be kind and available to her.

You'll see a thorough example of using this in Chapter 7.

A few examples of disqualifiers:

"I can already tell we'll not get along."

"You're fired!" (Say this like Trump from the *Apprentice Show*.)

"Oh, so you have a problem with guys who…?" (Mention a characteristic of yours.)

"I'm totally not boyfriend material."

"I'm the guy your mom warned you about."

"You can't handle a guy like me."

"I'm way too intense for you."

"You are way too inexperienced for me."

"How old are you? You are way too young for me."

"This has been great talking to you, too bad you're not my type…"

"You're too wimpy for me."

"That guy over there seems perfect for you."

"Your first impression sucks."

"You know what you're really bad at?" (Insert a comment about something bad.)

TOOL #4: SEXUAL TEASING/PUSHING HER TOWARDS YOU OR AWAY FROM YOU

A. Sexual Teasing

The goal in teasing is to create banter with a woman and engage her response to you. You tease a woman as a way to get her to react to you in a strong manner.

When you tease a woman you also **test** her. You test her response. Does she seem upset? Does she seem mildly interested in you? Is she laughing or avoiding you? If she is interested she will tease back or interact with you. If she's not interested she will avoid or ignore you.

One of the best things about teasing a woman is that you can introduce sexuality into a conversation in a silly manner. This can then set the tone for later sexual behavior and sexual interactions.

What's the point in seduction? Sex. A great way to move a conversation from platonic to sexual is to start introducing sexual teasing into an interaction.

Examples:

"Hey, turn around, I am going to spank you."

"You've been a bad girl, I'm going to punish you."

"Time for birthday spankings..."

"Let me see your lips, how often do you make out?"

"Do you like your nipple sucked or bitten?"

"Let's play spin-the-bottle."

"When was the last time you had sex?"

"If you had to fuck a guy in this bar, who would it be and why?"

"How long should a woman wait before having sex with a guy?"

"What is your porn star name?"

"What is your stripper name?"

B. Questions That Make Her Move Toward You

Up to this point we have been discussing ways to tease and bust women. We've avoided, however, offering suggestions for deeply personal questions to women where they have to work harder to get to know you. Complicated as it sounds, you need to ask women questions requiring that by merely answering the questions they begin the process of impressing you or coming closer to you. When you ask questions with negative assumptions, the woman then has to correct your negative assumption and therefore move toward you.

For example, if you ask a woman, "Is there more to you than just beauty?" she then will likely talk about how smart she is and explain to you ways in which she has accomplished things in life that are not based on beauty. Therefore, she is trying to impress you. She is moving toward you and proving herself to you. When she does this, you are then the hard to get one in the situation, not her.

Examples:

"Are you just another pretty face, or do you have depth too?

"Tell me something interesting about yourself."

"Do you only watch *Desperate Housewives* and *Sex in the City* or do you watch something with depth?"

"Do you even know what poetry is?"

"When I say the word 'philosophy,' what do you think of?"

"Are you interesting or boring?"

"Do you read books, or do you just rely on beauty to get through life?"

"Is there more to you than just beauty?"

"Is there more to you than meets the eye?"

"Did you even go to college?"

"What do you want to do when you grow up?"

CONCLUSION

You can see how these disconnectors would make a woman move toward you, while at the same time increasing your perceived value to her, thus making you Hard to Get.

Next we'll get into the "Big Guns"—the Heavy Disconnectors that you'll need to use in bar situations and with women who are especially hot or stuck-up.

118

CHAPTER 6

Heavy Disconnections

We saved the most hard-core stuff for last. This next section features our most street-level material. And we are strongly warning you right now that you'd better be very courageous and master the basic approach information before you try this stuff. Otherwise you're dead meat. By using heavy insults and heavily criticizing women, you open yourself up to some serious shit. You invite serious potential for conflict with a woman. In truth, you might even piss a woman off so badly that she gets some of her guy friends to kick your ass. You've been warned.

WHEN TO USE HEAVY DISCONNECTORS

If you're out with a great woman and things are fun and interesting and sexy, you do not need heavy disconnectors at all. You can skip everything in this section.

You use heavy disconnectors when the woman is being mean and nasty to you. You also use heavy disconnectors when the interaction is going really poorly and you do not know what else to do. You can use heavy disconnectors as a way to either get the interaction to succeed or to fail as a last resort, because you are going to drastically change it once you use a heavy disconnector. Things will either get ugly and bad fast or they will improve.

Heavy disconnectors can sometimes be helpful in the bedroom, as in a situation when you're not sure if you're going to have sex or not. The time just before sex can be awkward and full of mixed messages and uncertainty. Does the woman want to or not? Sometimes a heavy disconnector can help her make a strong decision.

TOOL #4: INSULTS

One of the most exciting things about picking up women is that you are interacting with strangers and you have no idea how the interaction will go: it's crazy and chaotic. As a result, you cannot sit around planning on how to respond to hypothetical situations. You need to go get your ass out there and get into situations and then react in an authentic way to things that happen to you. Again, when insulting someone you need to look at them and the situation and base your insult on real, live things that are happening.

Think about using insults this way: when you feel a woman needs to be punished for being snotty, mean, condescending, or rude to you it's time to INSULT her. It's time to punish her for being rude. You then let her know you're not a man who is

a supplicating puppy dog. You let her know that you have high self-esteem and that you are not a punching bag.

When you properly use insults with a woman you are giving her **blunt feedback** about her behavior. You are not letting her get away with rude actions or comments. In fact, it is actually strange and awkward when you let women do mean things and then simply choose to ignore their behavior.

Imagine if you were out with some buddies at a bar and some guy came into the bar and acted crazy. The guy screamed and drooled and broke a pool cue over a chair and then left. If this happened you would then talk about it. In fact, everyone in the bar would talk about it. It would be **all** anyone would want to talk about for a while, and then the turmoil would fade out and people would talk about other stuff.

Well, when a woman is rude and nasty it's sort of the same thing. When a woman is mean to you, she is well aware that she just acted that way. She also knows you are aware of it. So, if you do not say anything about her conduct it becomes odd for both of you. Instead, we recommend you talk to a woman in a blunt manner and bust her on her bad behavior. If you let her bad behavior slip too soon she will not respect you, the interaction will seem awkward, and you will be acting like a BNB and an Easy to Get Man. (We'll give you a lengthy, step-by-step example of this in the next chapter.)

There is a thin line between teasing and insulting a woman. When you purposefully insult a woman you are pushing her hard. You are putting things on the line with her and pushing her to either soften up, or go away.

Insult #1: You're the kind of person who...

This form of insult is when you bust a woman on her bad behavior. Whatever mean or rude thing she does, you tell her what you think in the form of a statement beginning, "You're the kind of person who."

You might say:

"You're the kind of person who feels superior to others and acts really snotty."

"You're the kind of person who acts aloof around men."

"You're the kind of person who is mean and nasty to strangers."

"You're the kind of person who sits in the corner alone and then gives guys shit when they try to talk to you."

"You're the kind of person who acts rude and nasty to get guys to go away and then complains that no one wants to date you."

"You're the kind of person who makes fun of guys just because they do not look like some Ken doll."

"You're the kind of person who is all nice and open and then gets all mean when someone asks for your phone number."

"You were one of those popular girls in school who thought she was better than everyone else and acted like a snotbag to everyone."

"You're the kind of woman who is really a stuck-up bitch."

"You're the kind of woman who dishes out the shit, but cannot take it when someone gives it right back."

Insult #2: You know what they say about girls who...

Another way of busting her on her bad behavior is to say, "You know what they say about girls who..." This pattern is most powerful when you fill in **real** stuff. Actually bust her on real things she has done or said to you that were truly offensive to you.

Say things like:

"You know what they say about girls who are mean to men."

"You know what they say about stuck-up women."

"You know what they say about women who are superattractive in their 20s."

"You know what they say about people who tease men who struggle with their careers."

"You know what they say about women who act nice and then suddenly act nasty."

"You know what they say about women who give dirty looks to men who come up and say hi."

Insult #3: I can't believe you said/did...

Yet another way of busting a woman is to say, "I can't believe you said or did [x]." Again, use real material when you bust a woman. It will be so much more powerful and real.

Say:

"I can't believe you just told me to get you a drink when we just met."

"I can't believe you told me to fuck off when I just said hi."

"I can't believe you just told my friend to get lost."

"I can't believe you called me a fat jerk when all I did was try to be nice to you."

"I can't believe you just put your hand in my face and told me to buzz off."

"I can't believe you just talked to me for 20 minutes and are now acting so snotty about giving me your number."

"I can't believe you are ignoring me after I got up the guts to come and talk to you."

Insult #4: Are you...

Another variation on the same theme of busting a woman on bad behavior is to ask her, "Are you..." This question is good because she must respond either by saying "yes" or "no" and then you can push things from there. This form of insult is good because it is direct and specific.

"Are you retarded?"

"Are you insane?"

"Are you crazy?"

"Are you really that nasty?"

"Are you on drugs?"

"Are you 12 years old?"

"Are you stupid?"

"Are you always this drunk and dumb?"

"Are you always so negative?"

"Are you always this much of a pain in the ass? How do your friends deal with you?"

"Are you always so bitchy?"

Insult #5: Busting a woman on being mean when you approach her

We created this list of insults to use specifically when you approach a woman and talk to her and she is rude, mean, or dismissive. These are pretty severe, but can be very effective in puncturing the bitch shield (much more on this in the next chapter).

Examples:

"Wow, you're harsh."

"Wow, you're rude."

"Are you always so rude?"

"Are you always this mean to strangers?"

"Did your mom teach you to be this nasty to people you don't even know?"

"Do you always leave a trail of dead bodies when you go out?"

"You must be a real hit at parties."

"It's no wonder you're single."

CONCLUSION

You now have every tool you need to know to create disconnections with women and to get them to move toward you, try to connect with you, and to pursue you.

Now let's put it all together, step-by-step, and give you some examples of how to use these tools in the real world.

CONCLUSION

You now have every tool you need to know to create disconnections with women and to get them to move toward you, try to connect with you, and to pursue you.

Now let's put it all together, step-by-step, and give you some examples of how to use these tools in the real world.

CHAPTER 7

Putting it All Together:
Your Exact, Step-by-Step Plan
for Being Hard to Get Today

You see a woman.

What do you do?

What DO you DO?!

We want to give you the most basic, brain-dead-simple approach to being "Hard to Get" that we possibly can.

The average man has one and only thought when he's interacting with a woman.

That thought is:

"How can I connect with this woman?"

As you know by now, that thought is WRONG, WRONG, WRONG.

Assuming that you know something about connecting with a woman already, here's the only 2 thoughts you need to have when you are interacting with a woman:

The first thought to have —> "Is it time to use a disconnector?"

When you decide that it is time to use a disconnector—and we are about to tell you how to do that—you go to the next question:

The second thought to have —> "What disconnector should I use?"

That's IT.

When you do properly timed and executed disconnects, you become the Hard to Get man that women pursue, and you set yourself apart from the legions of men who only try to connect.

And you can stop thinking about all that other junk that clogs your brain when you are talking to a hot woman.

We've given you everything you need to know... what you need to know now is EXACTLY how to apply it.

BEING A HARD TO GET MAN IN A BAR

Imagine that you are in a trendy bar and you see a woman who attracts you. She's superhot, and you watch as other men try to connect with her, and (predictably to you, now that you've read this book) you watch as those other men fail.

You want to approach her, but your mind freezes up with all the thoughts and concerns you have about approaching women.

Then you remember that we've made it simple for you: Remember the first thought the Hard to Get man has:

"Is it time to use a disconnector?"

If she's superhot and at a trendy bar on a Saturday night, she's likely to be pretty resistant to any man approaching her, especially someone whose looks are "average or below."

Remember, when a woman has too many men trying to connect to her, she needs a disconnect right away if she's going to have any interest in a man.

Taking Hard to Get actions is the best way to "get through to" a woman who has her bitch shield up.

So yes, it's time to do a disconnect... even before you do anything else. So you move on to the next question:

"What disconnector should I use?"

OVERCOME THE "BITCH SHIELD" AND BEING HARD TO GET WITH WOMEN IN BARS

You are more likely to have to overcome a woman's Bitch Shield if she is particularly hot, or in a place where she is being approached a lot.

More often than not, this location will be a **bar.**

When a woman has her bitch shield up she projects a hard, angry, bitter vibe. Most men try to get around that hostility, or pretend it isn't there. That makes them easy-to-get... and makes them failures with hot women.

The Hard to Get man confronts her behavior head-on.

Here's how our student Mike handled a woman go around a woman's Bitch Shield recently. You can follow these steps and do this too.

Mike was at a hot urban bar, and saw a beautiful young woman in pasha pants and a bikini top. She had breasts that could only be described as "alarmingly perfect" and "almost completely exposed." One by one men went up to her, and one by one she brushed them off in a brusque, angry way.

Mike, a practicing Hard to Get man, thought he'd take a try, too... but that he'd do things differently. While the other men he had watched approach her had found lame reasons to walk near her and then pretended to "notice" her, Mike walked right up to her.

Here are the steps he took. If you take them, too, you will get past a woman's Bitch Shield be a Hard to Get man.

Step 1: Disconnect by stating the truth about her.

Mike didn't start with "hi," or (God forbid) "You are really beautiful," or (extremely God forbid) "Can I buy you a drink," or any of the other lame things guys say.

He led with the truth. Which, in this case, was: "Wow, you look really angry."

This threw her off. This was different. She didn't like it, but at the same time, at least Mike wasn't being a groveling wimp like the other men.

"I not angry," She said. "I'm just sick of guys like you hitting on me."

How to do this step:

Pick at least one of these. Memorize it and practice it OUT LOUD until you can say it without even thinking:

"Wow, you look really angry."

"You look like you're having a bad day."

"You look bitter."

"You seem really nervous in social situations."

"You look great tonight, but there is something off about you."

Step 2: Accept her reaction to the truth.

Mike said, "Ah." And then waited.

Most men's knee-jerk reaction to such a negative response from a woman would be to try to "fix" the situation. They'd try to find something to say that would calm the woman down and make her like him.

Mike didn't do that. Instead, he let there be an uncomfortable silence for a few seconds. Actually, **she** was uncomfortable. Mike was fine, because he knew that allowing some brief discomfort made him a Hard to Get man.

How to do this step:

1) Remain calm. Keep breathing. Remember, this is making you Hard to Get, and laying the groundwork for her to pursue **you.**

2) Say "Ah."

3) Count off five seconds (by saying to your self "one-one-thousand, two-one-thousand, three-one-thousand, four-one-thousand, five-one-thousand).

Step 3: Do a "So you're the kind of woman who..."

After about 5 seconds, Mike said "So you're the kind of woman who is mean and nasty to strangers."

Let's talk about this step:

When you say something like this to a woman, you are simply feeding back to her how she appears to the world.

She has to either accept the truth of of what you said (which she won't want to do), or defend herself against it.

And when she starts defending yourself, you suddenly have a hot woman explaining herself to you.

And when a woman is explaining herself to you, she is has started down the path of pursuing you.

You are being a Hard to Get man.

How to do this step:

Pick at least one of these. Memorize it and practice it OUT LOUD until you can say it without even thinking:

"So you're the kind of woman who feels superior to others and acts really snotty."

"So you're the kind of woman who acts aloof around men."

"So you're the kind of woman who is mean and nasty to strangers."

"So you're the kind of woman who sits in the corner alone and then gives guys shit when they try to talk to you."

(Most women soften after being told one of these. If the woman you are talking to continues to be bitchy, continue to feed back her behavior to her with more "So you're the kind of woman who..." You can even use the same line over and over without changing it, as long as it's still true. If she continues to be a bitch, say matter-of-factly, "I thought you had a chance with me, but you really are a bitch, so I gotta go." Then leave.)

Now let's get back to our Hard to Get action with our student Mike:

When Mike told her "So you're the kind of woman who is mean and nasty to strangers," she didn't like it.

So she explained herself to Mike. "No," she said, "I'm just protecting myself."

At this point, a lot of men would get submissive and (again) try to diffuse the situation. They'd say something like "But I'm not that kind of guy!" Suddenly they'd be groveling-ly trying to connect again, and the woman would quickly get bored, or angry, or both— and move on.

"Containing" a Woman's Behavior

The key is **not** to avoid conflict with women. That's what all the Easy to Get men do, and by ignoring women's bad behavior, they end up groveling and alone.

But the key is also **not** to be defensive with women. That's what Impossible to Get men do, and they end up having fights with women, and that leaves them alone.

The key is to be able to **contain** the issue that is up between you and a woman without getting defensive or trying to fix what's going on.

And you are able to **contain** an interaction with a woman when you

1) Don't feel jerked around by a woman, and

2) Don't feel like you are groveling to a woman, desperately trying to connect with her.

These steps allow you to do that. When you do these steps with a woman, you won't feel jerked around, so you won't need to get angry and huffy, or to go crazy on her. You also won't feel like you are groveling or selling yourself you.

You'll be able to be present with the woman, no matter how she is behaving. And this will make you Hard to Get and desirable.

Step 4: Reward her by Complimenting her Conditionally

At this point, Mike's prospect had softened a little. She admitted what was really going on for her—that she was trying to protect herself from the onslaught of come-ons she was getting from men.

When a woman softens a little, and gets honest, you then give her a conditional compliment.

That's what Mike did next.

He said,

"That's okay, I like tough women. I thought you looked bitchy, but maybe you are nice."

Let's look at what he did here:

First, he complimented her on a real quality of hers: that she was tough.

But he also made it conditional by saying "I thought you looked bitchy, but maybe you are nice."

He gave her a compliment, but also reminded her of how she was appearing to the world.

Here's how she responded. She said, "It's just that I can't even go sit by the bar without all these guys coming up to me all the time with the most lame pickups."

At this point Mike got **curious**. "That's wild," he said. "What's the most clueless pickup line you get?"

"Oh God," She responded. "You wouldn't believe how many men come up to me and say, 'You are so beautiful.' Like I need to hear that a hundred times a day."

Mike said, "Ha! That's hilarious."

How to do this step:

There are two parts to this, but both parts are dirt simple.

Put as a formula, this step is made up of:

[compliment on some real quality of hers]+ [a condition, that the compliment only is true if she behave well].

Here it is broken out for you:

First—**compliment a real quality of hers that she was displaying, even though she was being a bitch.**

Memorize one or more of these:

"That's okay, I like women who are tough," or

"That's okay, I like women who are straight-up," or

"That's okay, I like a woman who's blunt with me."

Second—**make that compliment conditional on her continued good behavior.**

Memorize one of more of these:

"I thought you looked like a bitch, but maybe you are nice," or

"I thought you looked mean, but maybe you are okay," or

"I thought you looked bitter, but maybe you are okay."

So you end up saying something like, "That's okay, I like women who are tough. I thought you looked mean, but maybe you are okay."

Step 5: Create a Disconnect by Disqualifying Yourself

Most men—that is to say, the Easy to Get men, and your hapless competition—are trying to get women to judge them positively.

They are trying to qualify themselves to be with the woman by getting her to judge something nice about them.

This does not work on super-hot women in highly competitive environments.

As a Hard to Get man, you use her judgments of you—be they positive or negative—to "disqualify" yourself from being a man she'd be interested in... Thus making yourself harder to get.

HERE'S SOMETHING IMPORTANT YOU NEED TO KNOW ABOUT BEING A HARD TO GET MAN:

When you are being Hard to Get, you do not accept a woman's judgments of you—even if they are positive.

This is important. If you accept her judgments of you, then you put her in the driver's seat.

When a woman you desire makes a positive judgment about you, she is assuming that will want that positive judgment from her, and that you will gratefully (and submissively) accept it. That puts her back in the driver's seat, and suddenly you are looking for her approval again. Soon enough she will reject you, and go off looking for a harder-to-get man.

Equally, when a woman you desire makes a negative judgment about you, she is assuming you will want to change her mind about that negative judgment from her, and that you will vigorously (and submissively) refute it. Again, that puts her back in the driver's seat, as suddenly you are looking for her approval again. Again, soon she'll reject you, and go looking for a harder-to-get man.

Therefore, you have to turn the tables on her.

When she makes a positive judgment about you, you have to disagree with it.

And when she makes a negative judgment about you, you have to **agree** with it.

In this way you seem to "disqualify" yourself, and make the woman work to get to know you. You do this by seeming to "take yourself out of the game" of the pool of potential men for her.

So Mike then did a disqualifier. He said, "But here's the problem—I'm just one of those guys you never talk to, huh?"

She said, "No, you seem okay."

Again, most men would gratefully accept a hot woman's positive assessment of him. But not a Hard to Get man.

So Mike, who was 31, said, "Well, how old are you?" "Twenty-three," she replied.

"Oh, well, you're way too inexperienced for me."

This would be the end of the interaction if Mike let it be. But he went on.

How to do this step:

Pick at least one of these. Memorize it and practice it OUT LOUD until you can say it without even thinking:

If she's younger than you: "How old are you?" After she answers, say, "Oh, you're way to inexperienced for me."

"But here's the problem... I'm just one of those guys who [describe what she said she doesn't like], hun?"

"It's nice talking to you, but I'm totally not boyfriend material."

"It's nice talking to you, but I'm way too intense for you."

"It's nice talking to you, but we're way to different to get along."

"It's nice talking to you, but that guy over there seems perfect for you."

Step 6: Change Direction

If you simply disqualify yourself and leave it at that, she is likely to accept your disqualification. And that will be the end of the interaction.

So after you disqualify yourself, you have to keep the interaction **exciting** and **sexy** by changing direction.

A word about "changing direction" in an interaction with a woman:

Remember, the Hard to Get man is unpredictable. One minute he's upsetting, the next entertaining, the next serious, the next funny.

Easy to Get men try to avoid being unpredictable. In fact, the Easy to Get man wants to be as predictable and logical as he can be. This is a **huge mistake,** especially when you are interacting with in-demand, hot women.

We hereby free you from the constriction of being predictable and logical with hot women (after all, they don't feel the need to be predictable and logical with you!). You are now free to be illogical, unpredictable, and inconsistent with women.

You are free to change the subject from something deep to something silly, from something upsetting to something entertaining. We hereby give you permission!

At this point in his interaction, Mike needs to change direction (which you should always do after you "disqualify" yourself).

One way to do that is to ask a silly, wacko question. It's best if this question has some sort of sexual overtone, as it keeps the promise of sex in the situation, and keeps you from appearing like you truly have disqualified yourself.

You can do this by getting curious about something she says, or by using a "canned" redirection.

Getting back to our story...

After Mike said, "Oh, well, you're way too inexperienced for me," he knew it was time to change direction.

If she had responded with, "Oh, I don't know—I've done a lot for a woman my age," then Mike would change direction by getting curious, and asking her, "Really? What's something you've done that I'd be shocked by?"

This question—"What's something you've done that I'd be shocked by?"—changes the direction of the conversation toward something fun, wacky, and (potentially) sexy. Mike could continue to get curious about her answers, make jokes and tease her about the sexy thing she had done.

If she had responded more non-committally—which this woman did, with Mike, by saying, "Oh, okay," he would change direction by asking a Silly, Wacko question, which he did by asking the "canned" question, "Hey, here's a question: What would you do if you had a penis for a day?"

This opened up a sexually-oriented, silly and fun conversation between the two of them.

HOW TO "CHANGE DIRECTION" WITH A WOMAN

1) Be curious. Get curious about something she said, and ask a silly question about it. If she says, "I've done a lot for a woman my age," then ask her, "What's the most outrageous things you've done?" or "What have you done that would shock me?"

2) Ask a "canned" silly question. Use these to change direction if she hasn't said something to spark your imagination. **Memorize at least one of these questions, and practice it out loud until you can ask it easily at any time.**

"Hey, do you think vampires are sexy?"

"Hey, do you believe in ESP?"

"Here's a question... Have you ever put a hex on a guy when you were really mad?"

"Do you think things happen for a reason?"

"Hey, here's a question: What would you do if you had a penis for a day?"

"Do you believe in vampires?"

Have you ever been abducted by aliens?

Would you have sex with a ghost?

Are you into witchcraft?

Have you ever participated in a séance?

Do you know any friends who have been interested in the occult?

What's the craziest thing a guy has said to you?

Do you anyone who has been abducted by a UFO?

These questions may sound abrupt, but they change direction with the woman (which is an essential skill), and they introduce fun, silly topics of conversation.

Step 7: Be Curious, Continue to Use Disconnections as Needed

At this point, Mike had a connection established with this hot woman. She was interested in him, and had already done some work to connect with him, in response to his disconnections.

At this point, all Mike needed to do was stay with the interaction, continuing to disconnect when needed. He was way, waaay ahead of the Easy to Get men who were wishing they were him!

BAR BONUS TIP:

Here's a bonus tip about bars. When you are talking to a woman in a bar, your goal should be to have sex with her that night.

Put another way: The women you meet on the street, in bookstores, malls, or coffee shops, are usually not open to a new sexual experience right then.

Women in bars, on the other hand, often are.

A bar is a different, and in some ways "not real life" place for women, where they can behave in ways that they normally wouldn't indulge.

If you get a woman's phone number at a bar, that is better than doing nothing of course—but the next time you talk to her, she is likely to be in more of the "real life" mode, than the bar mode.

Meanwhile, when she is at the bar, she is more likely to be in the "do something outrageous now" mode that comes with drinking and partying and being out to have a good time. For that reason, you want to try to "close the deal" that night, if you can.

REVIEW: THE STEPS TO OVERCOMING A WOMAN'S "BITCH SHIELD" AND BEING HARD TO GET IN A BAR

Let's go over the steps he went through again:

Step 1: Disconnect by Stating the Truth About Her.

Mike told her the truth about how she appeared: "Wow, you look really angry."

Step 2: Accept Her Reaction to the Truth.

She got angry, and he said, "Ah," waited five seconds.

Step 3: Do a "So you're the kind of woman who..."

He then said, "So you're the kind of woman who is mean and nasty to strangers."

Step 4: Reward her by Complimenting her Conditionally

She soften in the face of this accusation, and started to defend herself to him, so mike said "That's okay, I like tough women. I thought you looked bitchy, but maybe you are nice."

If she had **not** softened, he would have done another "So you're the kind of woman who...", thus telling her more about herself.

In this case, she talked about how she was trying to defend herself from men who hit on her all the time.

Step 5: Create a Disconnect by Disqualifying Yourself

Mike stayed in the driver's seat by not accepting her judgments of him, whether they were positive or negative.

Mike said, "But here's the problem—I'm just one of those guys you never talk to, huh?" And when she said "No, you seem okay," he did **not** accept it... He asked her age, and then told her, "Oh, well, you're way too inexperienced for me."

Step 6: Change Direction

At this point if came back with, "I've done a lot for a woman my age," and could get curious, changing direction by saying, "What's something you've done that I'd be shocked by?"

He could also have asked a question seemingly "out of the blue," like, "Hey, what would you do if you had a penis for a day?" or one of the other outrageous questions we listed above.

Step 7: Be Curious, Continue to Use Disconnections as Needed

The conversation is happening, and all Mike has to do is to keep asking himself, "Is it time to use a disconnector?" and "What disconnector should I use?"

BEING A HARD TO GET MAN IN A DAY APPROACH

Now let's show you how to be a Hard to Get Man in daytime approaches.

The purpose of a daytime approach is to take the woman somewhere for a coffee date right then, or get her contact information so you can set up a date later. While "sex right now" on-the-street pickups do occur, the woman you meet on the street, in a bookstore, mall, or other "day" approach is more likely to be seduced over time than is the woman you meet in a bar.

Let's follow our student Jake as he uses his Hard to Get moves to get a woman to pursue him in a "day approach."

Jake was in a bookstore coffeeshop, when he saw a tall, statuesque and elegantly dressed woman who really caught his fancy (meaning she turned him on just to look at her). He decided to use his Hard to Get skills, and approached her.

1) Hook her interest

Day approaches are different than night/bar approaches in many ways, one of the most important being that you don't have to go in as aggressively or confrontational-ally. You can be aggressive and confrontational if you need to be, but most of the time you won't have to create the kind of big disconnects you need to get past a bar-babe's Bitch Shield.

When you want to hook a woman's interest in a day approach, you have three choices, with different levels of disconnect in each choice.

Choice 1: Say something Challenging

This is the most disconnecting level; thus it is the most risky, and also the level that will make her have to take the most action to explain herself to you (and thus move toward you).

There's a slight criticism in these challenging statements that she may feel she has to defend herself against. If she takes the bait (and she will. unless what you say is **too** critical of her), then she has to move toward you to change your slight negative opinion of her.

Saying something challenging is good for super-hot women who may be sick of being approached by puppy-dog, supplicating Easy to Get Men.

How to do this step:

Memorize these 2 "Mandatory" Opening Challenges. Practice them out loud until you can say them no matter how tongue-tied you may be:

"Wow, you look really bored."

"You look really lonely."

Which of these you say will vary on what is going on. If she looks wired on too much coffee, you wouldn't say "Wow, you look really bored." If you've watched her talk to ten people in the last five minutes, you wouldn't say "You look really lonely." But between these 2 Opening Challenges, you'll cover 90% of situations.

Additionally, you may want to memorize one of more of these:

"Wow, you look like you've been studying too long."

"Whoa, you look like you drank too much coffee."

"Why is your foot always moving when you are reading?"

"Do you know that your mouth moves when you are reading?"

With a little practice, you'll be able to make these up on the spot, and customize them to what is actually going on with the woman.

In this case, Jake decided to use this approach. The woman did indeed look bored, so he sat down at the table next to hers and said, "Wow, you look really bored."

Choice 2: Tease her using "Creative Misinterpretation."

We pioneered Creative Misinterpretation with women in "How to Succeed with Women." In that book we showed readers how to use Creative Misinterpretations to compliment a woman.

Now we'll show you how to use them to tease, challenge, and slightly disconnect with a woman.

You use Creative Misinterpretation with a woman when you make a joke about her, or the environment, based on a funny (and unlikely) misinterpreting of what she is wearing, doing, or something in the environment.

A Creative Misinterpretation puts a new (and often opposite) spin on something otherwise normal. If you are flirting with a cute female bank teller, for instance, you might say "Do you get to keep a percentage of the money that comes in? I bet you do."

The challenge here is that he has to join your world of joking and humor in order to communicate with you. She has to move toward you in the conversation, and be willing to accept your playful reality in order to interact with you at all. And that makes you an attractive man to her.

For instance...

If she's on a cell phone in a coffee shop, smile and say "Shh! This is a library, you know!"

If you are in a coffee shop using your computer, and she asks if she can plug hers in using the outlet under your table, smile and say, "Well, I don't know... There's only a limited amount of electricity, you know. I can't let you use any of mind unless I hear a really good reason first!

In Jake's case, there wasn't a readily-available misinterpretation he could make, so he didn't use this option.

Choice 3: Ask "What's the story behind that?"

"What's the story behind that?" is an immensely powerful flirting question (whether you use it to go for her phone number/email address or not). It relies on the fact that women think about the details of their appearance much more than you do, and they are likely to be wearing a piece of jewelry or article of clothing that is special to them.

When you ask about it, you touch into something personal for her. She'll want to talk about it, but it also might make her talk about something a little more personal than she normally would with a stranger. That is good.

After she's told you these details about her life, she's moved toward you by opening up to you.

When you are talking to a woman, be it a salesgirl behind a counter a woman at one of your Niches, or any woman at all, notice if she is wearing anything that looks unusual or personal. It might be a pin, a necklace, a piece of clothing, or a bracelet. Notice it, and ask her "What's the story behind that?" It's a powerful conversation-starter.

Ask about anything distinctive:

Glasses

Jacket or coat

How she's painted her fingernails or toenails

shoes

Pins or pendants

Rings

Necklaces

Stuff stuck in her hair

Odd materials of clothes

Bracelets

earrings

Strangely colored drink

Tattoos

Piercings

Handbag

Something she's carrying

You say it like this: "That's an interesting pin you are wearing. I've never seen one like it before. What's the story behind that?"

In this case, Jake might have approached his prospect and said,

"Hi. I noticed that interesting bracelet you are wearing. I've never seen one like it before, and I'm curious. What's the story behind that?"

In this case, Jake went with choice #1, saying, "Wow, you look really bored."

She immediately felt the challenge of it, and defended herself. "Not really," she said. I'm just spacing out because I've had a really busy day."

At this point Jake got **curious**—which is what you should do, too. He asked, "What have you been up to that wiped you out so much?"

She opened up to the question: "I had to have a client meeting, and was up all night prepping for it. It's like, if I don't get everything right, they don't buy, and I really want them to buy from me."

And the conversation was off!

2) Make yourself Scarce with a Time Constraint

A time constraint serves two purposes: It calms her anxiety about talking to someone new, and it makes you Hard to Get.

First, it calms her anxiety. Remember what we said before—when a woman is talking to a new man, she has two questions in her mind: "What is he going to do to me, and how long is it going to take?" When she knows that you are going to leave soon, she knows that you can't do much to her, because you won't be there long. This calms her, so you can get to know her better.

Second, it makes you a scare commodity, because you'll be gone soon. People want what is scarce, and in this interaction, that scare person is YOU.

How to do it:

"I only have only minute, but…"

"I'm with my friends, I can only stay a few seconds, so…"

"[Some other reason you have to go soon], but I had to say hello."

Jake said, "Well, I only have a few minutes here before I have to go, but I've had a challenging day, too. Let's spend a couple of minutes thinking about other things and cheer each other up!"

3) Ask "what's the story behind that" or a wacko question

If you didn't ask "What's the story behind that," you can do it now, right after you give her your time constraint.

You can also ask a wacky, silly question here. Depending on the vibe, the question can be anywhere from very sexual to not sexual at all.

Again, when you are being a Hard to Get Man with a hot woman at a bar, you are going to need to ask dramatic, outrageous, sexy wacko questions. In a day approach you will probably scale back the "wacko-ness" or the question to something that's more normal.

How to do this step:

Memorize (and practice out loud) 2 of these Silly, Wacko Questions for day approaches

"What's the craziest thing a guy has said to you?"

"Have you ever had an experience of ESP?"

"Here's a silly question—do you think people get abducted by aliens?"

"Do you believe in vampires?"

"Have you ever seen a ghost?"

"A friend of mine was just talking about this: Have you ever participated in a séance?"

More intensely and/or sexual:

"Hey, here's a question: What would you do if you had a penis for a day?"

"Would you have sex with a vampire?"

"Here's a question . . Have you ever put a hex on a guy when you were really mad?"

"Have you ever been abducted by aliens?"

"Would you have sex with a ghost?"

"Are you into witchcraft?"

Jake said, "So here's a silly question: Have you ever seen a ghost?"

This silly question took her mind off her troubles at work, and got her talking about something interesting, slightly intimate, and fun for her.

She started telling him about a time she was staying at a house in the country, and she saw a ghost in the bedroom, and so on.

4) Handle it if she's a bitch

While you will mostly do hard Bitch-Shield busting during night approaches in bars, you will sometimes encounter bitchy behavior during day approaches, too (though not nearly as often).

If she becomes a bitch, you can either just turn around and walk away (often the best choice, especially in a place where there are lots of available women to talk to), or you can use the same techniques with her you would use with a difficult woman in a night approach.

As in the night approach, you'd use a Truth Disconnect or a Canned Disconnect. You might say, "Wow, that was a really mean thing to say. Didn't your Mother teach you how to be polite to stranger?" or "Holy shit, you're really rude to strangers," or "You must really be a hit at parties," or "Do your friends know how rude you are?"

Then you'd simply follow the "Night Approach" steps of Accepting Her Reaction to the Truth, doing a "So you're the Kind of Woman Who...," Conditionally Complimenting her if she deserves it, and then getting on with the "Day Approach" steps listed here.

Remember this: If things are going well with a woman on a day approach, you limit the number of disconnections that you do. If things are really going well, you have great chemistry, and she's being really sweet to you, there's no reason to disconnect. Take the good times as far as they will go. If she becomes a bitch at some point, disconnect with her. Otherwise, ride the success as far as it will go!

5) Have some "Fluff talk."

While you often have to stick to intense, confrontational and outrageous talk in a loud bar with a woman who is in high demand, during a day approach you will at some point simply chit-chat about random, non-seductive things.

Get curious about her life. Ask her questions, and share stories about your own life and experiences.

How to be a Hard to Get Man during "Fluff Talk"

Most men mess up "Fluff talk" by suppressing the truth about themselves. They become overly agreeable (or become a jerk when they do disagree).

Fundamentally, you must be willing to have differences with the woman you are talking to, and you must be willing to resist the twin temptations of glossing over those differences or being a jerk about them.

You must be willing to all there to be disagreements between you. For instance, as Jake Fluff-Talked with his prospect, she mentioned that she hated football. Jake actually **played** football with friends on weekends, and really enjoyed it.

He didn't hide this difference. He didn't try to gloss over it. And he didn't try to make it a bigger deal than it was. He simply said,

"Oh, that's too bad. I play football with my buddies on a regular basis. I really love it."

Then he changed the subject, and moved on with the conversation.

Remember: **Differences and disagreements you have with a woman are not "issues" that you need to resolve or "process" together.** They are differences that make you interesting and more of a Hard to Get Man.

6) Close The Deal

There are 2 kinds of day-approach closes.

First—Keeping it short, getting her contact info, and following up later.

Most of the time, you will get the best day-approach Hard to Get-Man results by keeping the interaction slightly shorter than she might want, getting her contact info, and getting out of there while you both are still having fun.

Put another way... You **don't** want to be one of those men who stays around a woman until you've finally bored her into having to leave. Get out first and you become a Hard to Get Man.

How to do it:

If you used a time-constraint at the beginning, you can return to it now.

This is what Jake said to "close" his prospect: "Wow, I really do have to be going right now. But this has been a lot of fun... What would it be like if we got together for a cup of coffee sometime?"

You then:

1) Get her phone number and/or

2) Get her email and/or

3) Set up a time and place before you leave, so you can meet up later without having to set up the date on the phone or via email.

That's the scenario you'll follow most of the time. You'll leave while it's still fun, and get her info to follow up with her later.

You'll leave while she's wishing you'd stay around, once again creating a disconnect that draws her to move toward you and pursue you.

Or...

Second—Move the date into a full seduction right then, and either take her to another seductive venue, and eventually to a place where you can have sex. You may go on a romantic walk, a dinner date, a rock concert, or even directly back to your home.

This sometimes does happen with day approaches, but it's not nearly as common as night approaches. Remember, if you **don't** have sex with a woman you meet at a bar on the night you meet her, the likelihood of ever having sex with her goes down dramatically.

That's emphatically **not** true in day approaches, where the odds of having sex with right away are small, but the odds of developing a sexual relationship later are much much greater.

Review: The Steps to being Hard to Get in Day Approaches

Step 1: Hook Her Interest

You can do this by saying something challenging, Teasing her with Creative Misinterpretations, or asking "What's the Story Behind that?"

Jake decided to say something challenging: "Wow, you look really bored."

Step 2: Make Yourself Scarce with a Time Constraint

When you first approach a woman, she wants to know "What's he going to do to me, and how long is it going to take?" You remove fear from the situation, while making yourself more valuable, by using a time-constraint.

Jake said, "I only have few minutes here before I have to go, but..."

Step 3: Ask "What's the Story" or a Wacko Question

Now it's time to get interesting and playful. Jake asked a wacko question: "Have you ever seen a ghost?"

Step 4: Handle it if She's a Bitch

Use the techniques from the "Being a Hard to Get Man in a Bar" section if she becomes a bitch as you talk to her.

Step 5: Have some "Fluff Talk"

Not all conversation is a direct line to seduction; some of the conversation, especially during a day approach, is just the low-impact experiencing of one another.

The critical thing in fluff talk is to allow there to be differences and disagreement between you, without ignoring it or overfocusing on it. When his prospect said she hates football, Jake said, "That's too bad. I play football with my buddies on a regular basis."

Step 6: Close the Deal

Return to your time-constraint, and either go to another venue with her right then, or (more likely) get her contact information so you can continue the seduction later.

Jake said, "Wow, I really do have to be going right now. But this has been a lot of fun... What would it be like if we got together for a cup of coffee sometime?"

By this point he had disconnected from her enough, and in the right ways, that she was interested in seeing him again as soon as he could manage it.

NOW USE THIS IN YOUR LIFE!

There may be times that using all this seems complicated. If so, remember the basic tools of disconnection: Truth disconnects and Canned Disconnects.

Remember the only two thoughts a Hard to Get Man is having at any given moment:

The first thought to have —> "Is it time to use a disconnector?"

When you decide that it is time to use a disconnector—and we are about to tell you how to do that—you go to the next question:

The second thought to have —> "What disconnector should I use?"

And remember, you can use disconnection at any time it's needed in an interaction with a woman, to any degree of intensity the situation calls for.

For instance, our student Dennis was on a first date with a woman he met at the school where he was a graduate student. She was 25 years old and very attractive, and he was concerned that she had coasted by on her good looks. He suspected that he'd need to disconnect from her, but at first there wasn't any need to: She was attentive and interesting and they got along well.

They were sitting at dinner when the moment finally came. Her cell phone rang. She took it out of her pocket, and without even looking to see who it was, answered it.

And had a five-minute conversation.

Through her entire conversation, Dennis just looked at her. He wasn't looking at her with rage, and he wasn't seething. He was looking at her with what might be called a "look of judgment."

He knew it was time to do a disconnect. So he decided to do a Truth Disconnect.

He was angry, but he remembered that the point of a Truth Disconnect was **not** to be a crazy pissed-off jerk that she could (and should) easily dismiss. He remembered that the point of a Truth Disconnect was to confront her with the truth of her own bad behavior.

So when she finally hung up the phone, he didn't yell. He didn't seethe. But he didn't smile, either.

He simply told her the truth about herself. He looked at her and said, "You have the worst cell phone manners of anyone I've ever met."

Then he waited.

He knew that if she tried to attack him, at that point, he could always go to a "So you're the kind of person who...," which would diffuse her attack.

He didn't jump in to try to get rid of the sense of tension that what he said put into the space. He waited, in that discomfort, for what she'd say next.

After a very long five seconds of neither of them seeming to breathe at all, she let out a long exhale and said, "Wow, I'm really sorry. I didn't realize I was being rude, I didn't think the call would take so long. Here, I'm turning it off." She then turned off her cell phone.

He then went to a conditional compliment. "Ok, that's good. I like a woman who can turn off her cell phone. I thought maybe you were just a rude woman, but maybe I was wrong." Then without missing a beat, he picked back up the conversation they were having before her cell phone call came in.

By taking this Hard to Get action, Dennis separated himself from the Easy to Get Men who would have simply taken her bad behavior, or the Impossible to Get Men who would have caused a scene about it. He showed his value and, more importantly, made her value him as well. He made her move toward **him**, and pursue a connection with **him.** Dennis had sex with her that very night.

We expect that, by this point, you are starting to see how you can use the tools of being a Hard to Get Man in your interactions with women. You, too, can be like Dennis. You now have everything you need to start practicing getting the women you desire to approach you by being a Hard to Get man.

Please send us your questions and stories of your successes to ronanddavid@howtosucceedwithwomen.com.

HERE IS A SAMPLE OF TH
GET WHEN YOU GO TO

Men, especially shy men, don't do disconnectors because they get too worried about what might happen. They imagine all sorts of results that are so bad that they can't ever take action at all. But here's something you need to understand...

No matter how "nice" you think you are, if you don't have the success with women that you want, you are actually a lot more "disconnecting" with women than you think.

You see, a lot of the things men do to try to be "nice" are actually so tired, so fake, and so grovel-y that they push women away EVEN WORSE than a real, seductive disconnector would do.

Yet guys think they aren't disconnecting, even when they persist in being shy, or saying things like "You're so beautiful," or groveling to women.

MYTHS ABOUT USING DISCONNECTORS

MYTH #1: **Disconnectors are attacks on women.** Actually, a disconnector (even a harsh one, if it is done in our method) is an interesting invitation for a woman to engage with you on deeper, more authentic level.

But they are disconnecting with women—only not seductively at all. Let's be crystal clear: If you are NOT doing seductive disconnectors, and you are NOT getting what you want with women, you ARE pushing women away...

So you might as well do a seductive disconnector instead.

To read about the other myths and get more useful information about using Disconnectors go to this site:

HTTP://HOWTOSUCCEEDWITHWOMEN.COM/HTG2222840.HTML

ORTS OF BONUSES YOU

HTTP://HOWTOSUCCEEDWITHWOMEN.COM/ HTG2222840.HTML

MYTH #2: If you use a disconnector with a woman, it will ruin her day, or hurt her in some way. It's actually your unwillingness to be an interesting challenge to a woman that makes her life boring and annoying. This is your chance to be different!

MYTH #3: If you use a disconnector, you'll end up in a huge conflict with the woman.

"Breakout Session" #1   howtosucceedwithwomen.com/htg

BE "HTG"

Get the women you desire to pursue you by being a "Hard to Get" Man.

Here's how to do your VERY FIRST DISCONNECTOR with a hot woman

BONUS BREAKOUT SESSION #1: HOW TO DO YOUR VERY FIRST "DISCONNECTION" WITH A HOT WOMAN

This Breakout Session's purpose is to coach you through the process of doing your very first disconnection with a woman. This is also available as an audio!

Get your "Hard to Get Man" bonuses (worth over $100.00) when you get this book...

When you buy "How to Be the Bad Boy Women Love" you are eligible for special extra "Hard to Get Man" bonuses, including... *How to Do Your First "Disconnect" with a Hot Woman*

This bonus "break-out session" will take you by the hand and walk you step-by-step through doing your FIRST disconnection with a woman.

This special report and 2 downloadable audios covers...

* Overcoming the myths that stop you from using disconnectors with hot women;

* Real-world examples of successful "first disconnections" with hot women;

* How to prepare yourself for doing your first disconnector with hot women;

* Handling her reaction to your disconnection;

... and more.

You'll also get access to other special info and updates!

Once you've got the book, grab yours by going to

HTTP://HOWTOSUCCEEDWITHWOMEN.COM/HTG2222840.HTML